The Political Economy of
Public Organizations

The Political Economy of Public Organizations

A Critique and Approach to the Study of Public Administration

Gary L. Wamsley

Mayer N. Zald

INDIANA UNIVERSITY PRESS
BLOOMINGTON AND LONDON

First paperback edition published 1976 by Indiana University Press

Copyright © 1973 by D.C. Heath and Company

Published in Canada by Fitzhenry & Whiteside Limited,
Don Mills, Ontario

Manufactured in the United States of America

LIBRARY OF CONGRESS CATALOGING IN PUBLICATION DATA

Wamsley, Gary L.
    The political economy of public organizations.
    First published by Lexington Books, Lexington, Mass.
    Includes bibliographical references and index.
    1. Public administration. 2. Organization. I. Zald, Mayer N., joint
author. II. Title. JF1351.W35 1976   350   76–10485
ISBN 0–253–34525–1 pbk.   1 2 3 4 5 80 79 78 77 76

Contents

List of Figures and Tables

Preface

This extended essay grew out of our discontent with the current state of public administration theory. The essay also grew out of our belief that the recent development of the political economy approach to organizations by one of us* might solve some of the major conceptual problems of the field of public administration.

Both of us, from different vantage points, had long lamented the state of public administration theory. As a teacher and student of public administration, Wamsley long had believed that theory in this field was a hodgepodge of ideas and approaches, semivalid prescriptions, and exhortative homilies. As a student of complex organizations and political sociology, Zald had believed much of the scholarship in the field was based on inadequate organizational analysis and theory. Both of us believed that the study of *public* administration had to have organic links to political science and political analysis. At the same time we both believed that its focus upon administrative management of public agencies required organic links to organizational theory. The political economy approach meets these requisites. It is an approach to the study of organizations that is congenial with political science and has explicit political concepts and analyses.

Although the initial statement of our general framework had been developed by Zald, both of us share the responsibility for its application here. After several discussions and outlining sessions, Zald drafted a short manuscript. From that point Wamsley took the lead in expanding and rewriting the several drafts. Although both of us take responsibility for the final product, Wamsley, deserves the major credit for making the book relevant to students of public administration.†

Several scholars have aided us by their encouraging but acerbic comments. Organizational analysis flourishes in the rich environment of Vanderbilt, and we are indebted to our colleagues John Dorsey, George Graham, Leiper Freeman, Avery Leiserson, Lee Sigelman, James D. Thompson, and Benjamin Walter for their comments on earlier drafts. We are also heavily indebted to Philip Kronenberg, of Indiana University, and Dwight Waldo of Syracuse University.

When this manuscript was written Mayer Zald held a Research Scientist Development Award (K34,919) from the National Institutes of Mental Health (USPHS).

The first chapter states fully our discontent with the current state of public

---

*Mayer N. Zald, "Political Economy: A Framework for Comparative Analysis," in POWER IN ORGANIZATIONS, M.N. Zald, ed. (Nashville, Tenn.: Vanderbilt University Press, 1970), pp. 221-61, and Mayer N. Zald, ORGANIZATIONAL CHANGE: THE POLITICAL ECONOMY OF THE YMCA (Chicago: University of Chicago Press, 1970).

†A summary article has been published. Gary L. Wamsley and Mayer N. Zald, "The Political Economy of Public Organizations," PUBLIC ADMINISTRATION REVIEW, vol. 33, No. 1 (Jan/Feb 1973), 62-73.

administration theory, sketchily reviews alternative approaches, and briefly outlines the political economy approach. Chapters 2 and 3 then detail the major dimensions and concepts of the framework, along the way illustrating their applicability to local, state, and national administration. Chapter 2 focuses upon the environment or external political-economic relations, structures, and processes of public agencies, while Chapter 3 focuses upon their internal political-economic structure. The final chapter addresses itself to some of the discreet traditional (e.g., civil service reform) and modern (e.g., administration in developing nations) concerns of public administration. Its purpose is to show how the political economy approach synthesizes, unifies, and illuminates traditional concerns.

G.L.W. Lawrence, Kansas

M.N.Z. Nashville, Tennessee

The Political Economy of
Public Organizations

A Fragmented Field in Need of Theory

The search for a theory of public administration over the decades has taken on aspects of a quest for the Holy Grail or a hunt for the mythical unicorn. The search has been filled with zeal and piety, but seldom has it been made clear what it is that is sought, nor have the searchers been altogether certain of its existence. Public administration theory (PAT) is a term used with incredible looseness. "Theory" has meant variously: a search for "scientific principles"; efforts to refute the existence of such principles; broad ruminations about what phenomena are included within the rubric public administration; general orientations of students of public administration, whether professional and "applied" or academic and "pure."

One of the principal reasons why the term "theory" has been so abused in public administration has been the schizoid nature of the field. On the one hand, there has been a pulling and hauling over something called "politics," which apparently has to do with questions of legitimacy and conflict; and, on the other hand, there has been the concern for "management," which apparently has to do with achievement of maximum efficiency. We hope to set forth a conceptual framework that can bring these two divergent concerns together in the process of building a scientific and empirical theory of the phenomenon called "public administration."

If the study of public administration is ever to become a part of social science, the word "theory" must be used in a more stringent sense than it has been.[a] True enough, for several decades political scientists have exhorted their brethren to rigor and science, but in the study of public administration appeals to science and rigor have seldom gone beyond exhortation.

Although there are no generally accepted steps for developing scientific theory, once the task of developing a theory is undertaken, certain requirements must be satisfied. A useful theory must have operational concepts specifying significant variables. The researcher also must have at his disposal some notions about how variables relate and why they are significant. This effort to "make some sense of it" is often a mere guessing game of probable relationships. The effort, however, is greatly facilitated if there is available a framework, or conceptual scheme, which both provides guidelines for hypotheses and links many problems under a single theoretical rubric. Proof of a hypothesis so linked

---

[a]G.C. Homans, "Bringing Man Back In," AMERICAN SOCIOLOGICAL REVIEW V, 29, no. 6 (December 1964): 809-18. We believe with Homans that the purpose of theory is to explain by interrelated and proven propositions that answer the question "Why?"

to other propositions gives support to acceptance of a unifying paradigm and, in turn, leads to the paradigm's further heuristic utility.[1]

Sometimes the explanations produced by theory will be used in an applied or prescriptive manner. Whether such use is good or bad depends on one's attitudes toward the results of the application. In social science normative and ideological considerations often play a part both in shaping the underlying assumptions of a paradigm and in defining a particular phenomenon as a "problem" needing explanation. And probably some students of the phenomenon or "problem" anticipate normative application of findings. If kept in proper perspective, normative uses of theory and research need not invalidate or hamper explanation of a phenomenon. They become a problem only if they divert attention from collective efforts at theory building or outrun understanding produced by theory. Much to the detriment of the field, in some of its guises PAT has been mainly an attempt to state right principles of administration.[b]

But if we are to develop a scientific public administration we need a framework to guide our efforts. According to Thomas Kuhn, at some point a paradigm is accepted in the scientific study of a phenomenon.[2] A paradigm represents a consensus for a field of inquiry. It provides decision rules for a discipline, and sets out a logic or conceptual map by which one proceeds to analyze and from which one draws inferences. It creates and is created by a distinctive coherent research tradition. Basic tenets of the field remain unquestioned while work is limited to the solution of paradigmatic puzzles. According to Kuhn this stage is a sign of maturity in a particular scientific field. Clearly, then, a paradigm is more global and overarching than a model and, although less precise, it provides the framework for model building and testing. The paradigmatic puzzle solving leads to theory. As Landau points out:

A pre-paradigmatic stage offers a striking contrast to a normal science (which is reflected by a paradigm). The discipline . . . so called . . . is marked by a plethora of competing schools, a polyglot of languages, and accordingly, a confusion of logics. There is neither a common research tradition nor the necessary consensus for a common field of inquiry. Each of the competing schools questions the others, adventurism is rampant, and commonly accepted standards of control do

---

[b]Many students of public administration have decried the lack of scientific theory. See Robert A. Dahl, "The Science of Public Administration: Three Problems," PUBLIC ADMINISTRATION REVIEW (Winter, 1947): 1-11. The instances of prescriptive norms outrunning theory are so diffuse and widespread that it is difficult to specify. Some would cite the recommendations of the 1937 Brownlow committee and the two Hoover commissions as examples of major governmental changes based on prescriptive principles that had little solid base in science. Although the commissions may have done some good, they failed to solve many problems and exacerbated others. Herbert Simon has given the best critique of some of the field's prescriptive norms in his ADMINISTRATIVE BEHAVIOR (New York: Free Press, 1965), Chap. 2. The current generation of students of public administration are only slightly, if any, less prescriptive than their predecessors. They have a general bent toward prescribing, offering consultant services, or "intervening" in the subjects they study.

not exist. This stage can be preliminary to a science, or it can appear as a temporary condition which follows upon the rejection of common paradigm.[3]

This seems an uncomfortably apt description of the study of public administration.

The time seems ripe for efforts at building an empirical theory of public administration. We agree with Philip S. Kronenberg that such a theory must rest on (1) agreement on specifications of the field of inquiry, (2) the extent to which phenomena of the field are linked in a system of explanations, (3) a high quality of empirically explicit operational concepts with replicable findings and explanatory power.[4] This essay cannot begin to present such a theory. Yet, hopefully it does more than piously call for one. It is intended to set forth a framework[c] that is simple, yet with enough heuristic power to make its application to a wide range of students of public administration; a framework around which existing and new studies and concepts can be organized, and which might therefore serve as a paradigm—a prelude to theory development.

Defining the Field of Public Administration

After decades of debate students of public administration are still mired down in a boundary problem, indicating a lack of coherent focus for the subject. Since this work proposes a framework for theory building in *public* administration we must address the issue of whether a meaningful and useful distinction can be made between public and private administration, and of whether the field has intellectual coherence.

It is not possible to "swallow the world whole" and since political scientists seek to understand the political and governmental system, simple pragmatism might lead one to make a distinction between public and private administration. Even in societies that have minimally differentiated governmental structures, the operation of the political system is strongly dependent upon offices and agencies that claim to act authoritatively for the whole society for the definition, development, and execution of public policy. Thus, political scientists interested in these societies must include analysis of these agencies if they are to understand the operation of the political system.

It might be granted that to understand the political system one must understand how public agencies operate. Yet, from at least two perspectives, it is possible to deny that public administration as an intellectual discipline has any

---

[c]We often use the word "framework" rather than "paradigm" because, as described by Kuhn, a paradigm is a set of integrated ideas and assumptions that are well *accepted* by a group of scholars. Although our work synthesizes much work, it is not well accepted. In a sense we are proposing a framework that we would like to see become an accepted paradigm.

special theoretical focus. On the one hand, if one is interested in administration-qua-administration, or organization-qua-organization, then making a distinction between public and nonpublic administration may be counterproductive, blinding the analyst to the essential similarities in structure, function, and process.[d] On the other hand, if one is mainly interested in the operation of political systems but believes that public agencies are essentially the same as other organizations, it is necessary merely to turn to the organizational or management literature for the tools of analysis to be used for understanding this specific part of the political system. In other words, one would "plug in" variables and concepts from organizational analysis in attempting to examine the functions of government and the legitimacy and effectiveness of regimes.

It is our position, however, that public organizations have distinctive characteristics that make the study of public administration a separable but interrelated discipline, and, if it is to be well developed, contributing to the aims of political science as well as to more traditional, practical ends, it must have organic links to political science and to organizational analysis.

If we try to understand the operation of public agencies and treat some aspect of public organizations as a dependent variable, as something to be explained, we will find that, in the main, public agencies are subject to a different set of constraints and pressures than private ones. Organizational variables take on different weights in the public sector. Additionally, if we are interested in the effectiveness and legitimacy of regimes and if we treat public policies and the agencies that implement them as independent variables affecting legitimacy and effectiveness, then we need an understanding of the political processes—an understanding which is quite different from that needed to comprehend the impact of private organizations on public policies—and the part played by agencies in these processes. The whole concept of organizational effectiveness—and effects must be approached differently in the public and private sector. It is our contention, therefore, that for both pragmatic and

---

[d]One academic effort at breaking down the boundary has come from organizational sociologists who assert that administration is a phenomenon found in both public and private spheres. Thus they say a theory should be developed largely ignoring sector lines. The function of such a theory would be to "offer a more precise description of administration and ultimately facilitate the prediction of administrative events in unknown but conceivable circumstances." See James D. Thompson et al., COMPARATIVE STUDIES IN ADMINISTRATION (Pittsburgh, Pa.: Pittsburgh University Press, 1959), p. 3. Thompson and his collaborators seek the variables that make a difference. If underlying the public-private distinction were important factors shaping differences in organizations, these factors should be part of a general approach to organizations. We agree with their argument. Indeed, it is our contention that critical, relevant variables of public organizations often take different "weights" and that these variables cluster together to differentiate public from private organizations. For us, it is important to highlight these clusters and differences.

For earlier writers who play down the difference see L. Urwick and Luther Gulick, eds., PAPERS ON THE SCIENCE OF ADMINISTRATION (New York: Columbus University, Institute of Public Administration, 1937); and more recently, Edward H. Litchfield, "Notes on a General Theory of Administration," ADMINISTRATIVE SCIENCE QUARTERLY 8 (9 June 1956).

theoretical reasons public administration ought to be a hybrid discipline linking, at a minimum, organizational analysis and political science.

Difficulties in Distinguishing Public and Private

But asserting that a discipline has a distinctive focus and living with such a distinction are different matters indeed. Students of public administration have tried, but the results have been disappointing. At first glance the definitional problem is deceptively simple: public administration is the study of the administration of state activities. In essence this position is correct. However, there are subtleties and complications in the real world that make its simplicity deceptive.

There are two major varieties of problems which lead some scholars to want to ignore the distinction between public and private administration. First, the activities of the state encompass such a conglomeration of structural forms and diverse functions that it is often difficult to ascertain the common elements of public organizations. Each function is alleged to have distinctive aspects to its administration. Students are often lured into eclectic probing that earns them the label of dilettantes.[5]

The second major difficulty in maintaining the conceptual purity of public administration is the interpenetration of government and business. The symbiotic relationship, for example, between the U.S. Air Force and Lockheed Corporation, on the one hand, and the government controls over Lockheed's operations, on the other, has resulted in a blurring of whatever lines of demarcation might have existed between public and private sectors. Moreover in many countries the state may "own" most organizations of any consequence, rendering the distinction empirically empty.

Dahl and Lindblom's classic study showed clearly how private, quasi-governmental, and governmental organizations tend to shade imperceptibly into one another.[6] But their main point, it seems, is *not* that distinctions between public and private are meaningless, but merely that assertive, pejorative, or prescriptive demarcations are meaningless.

They make a distinction between agency and enterprise. An enterprise is an organization (public or private) which is more responsive to a price system than an agency (public or private) which is more responsive to polyarchy or hierarchy, i.e., various political constraints.[7] They note the following differences between public and private organizations. Public organizations

—are controlled more by superiors or other political actors than they are by a price system;
—must cope with funding that is more highly contingent upon previous experience and perceptions of superiors;
—tend to have more vaguely defined or multiple goals, among which cost reduction does not receive very high priority;

—are relatively insulated from automatic penalties and rewards of the price system;

—generally lack objective tests of efficiency by product or service;

—are able at times to shift their costs to other agencies rather than face them or go under;

—are not generally provided by cost reduction with opportunity for growth.[8]

It will become apparent that key aspects of the political economy paradigm are similar to the agency-enterprise distinction of Dahl and Lindblom. Organizational behavior and outputs vary with the particular blend of politicoeconomic control or constraints. But where their broad purposes lead them to ignore the line between public and private the effort in this work is to find a way to observe it! Moreover, a device like the political economy framework would meet a real need if it could handle the subtleties, problems, and distinctions between organizations *but* do so within the public sector.[e]

If there is difficulty in drawing a clear boundary between public and private, what is distinctive about the public sector that makes building a theory of public administration a meaningful strategy of knowledge accumulation? The major features distinguishing public and private organizations are found in basic differences in the political bases of organizations and in their mechanisms of economic resource procurement.

Political and Economic Bases of Definition

A government is a system of rule, and it is distinctive from nongovernmental institutions in that (1) it ultimately rests upon coercion and a monopoly of force, and (2) if legitimate, it speaks for the society as a whole; if not, it purports to do so. From these fundamental features flow definitions of membership, rights, expectations, and obligations in relation to the state or ruling regime of a society (and its organizations). The concept of a polity, of a political system, implies a differentiation of governmental institutions from other institutions, e.g., religious, familial. Although every society has political structures and functions—mechanisms for mobilizing the society for collective purposes and for resolving intergroup conflicts and demands—only as institutions differentiate, as roles and organizations become separate from lineage structures, does it become meaningful to speak of a distinctive polity and government.[f]

Because public organizations are part of the state, citizens develop distinctive

---

[e]Though we are emphasizing its applicability to public organization, we think the framework may have value for analyzing all organizations regardless of sector; it clarifies differences among private organizations, between public and private organizations, and among public organizations.

[f]Obviously, one can speak of the "governing" of a family or of the politics of small groups to refer to the system of authority rule and conflict resolution in these micro-social systems.

expectations and perceptions of public agencies. As Murray Edelman notes, state actions are perceived of as having important, continuing, and direct consequences for a group (benefiting and hurting, threatening and reassuring).[9]

Politics is for most of us a passing parade of abstract symbols, yet a parade which our experience teaches us to be a benevolent or malevolent force that can be close to omnipotent. Because politics does visibly confer wealth, take life, imprison and free people, and represents a history with strong emotional and ideological associations, *its processes become easy objects upon which to displace private emotions, especially strong anxieties and hopes.*[10]

This relation to political action arises from the unusual aspects of legitimacy and coercion that grow out of the function of a political system. It is the political system with public agencies at its heart that authoritatively and legitimately (or claiming these qualities) allocates resources, or rewards, or deprives in order to maintain society's cohesion and direction, and brings about alterations in that direction. The state is associated with the survival of the people: and only the state can legitimately, in the name of society as a whole, apply the ultimate sanctions of death or incarceration. It is not surprising, therefore, that the state and its agent organizations, whether police, bureaus, or courts, are perceived as having a different significance for the lives of citizens than do private organizations. This perception of significance has the potential to affect even the most hum-drum activities of government by organizations that are public merely by historic accident.[11]

When the Christmas rush becomes too heavy for the archaic post office and the system breaks down, or a strike erupts, as in 1970, the army is called upon to deliver the mail. And tampering with the mail brings the FBI to the scene.

The distinctive relation of citizens to the public sector can be seen at work when the government "takes over" a task previously performed by private organizations. An excellent example can be found in Simon, Smithburg, and Thompson, even though they attempt, for reasons of their own, to play down the difference between the public and private sectors:[12] During World War II the government had to seize the coal mines to insure production in the face of a threatened strike. The only tangible change was the hoisting of an American flag over the mines and the appointment of an army officer to run the mines. The miners returned to work under the same management and conditions, but with changed attitudes towards their work. Such a distinction between public and private was relatively unimportant for Simon, Smithburg, and Thompson, owing to the thrust of their work, but it is crucial for our purposes, for both citizens and public organizations hold expectations of one another that usually cannot be found in the transactions between private organizations and citizens.

Out of the citizen's perceptions of the significance of state action—the shadow of state power to incarcerate or execute—and perceptions about rights and obligations grow distinctive concerns about the legitimacy of a public organization's existence or mode of operation. Public organizations are perceived as "belonging to," or as "owned by," the state and the citizenry. Thus, a major distinction between public and private organizations is a *political* one. Out of the penumbra of sovereignty and authority that surrounds them develops a distinctive pattern of legitimate use, disposal, and allocation of organizational resources. Public organizations are *"owned"* by the state claiming to represent society as a whole; enfranchised citizens and ruling elites have "rights" and "expectations" that derive from a public organization's relation to the state. Private organizations are perceived of as being "owned" by individuals or groups that have earned or been given rights of use. In private organizations sovereignty vests not in the government but in whichever individuals or groups are accredited by the society as owners.

To be sure, the distinction between public and private sovereignty is not clearcut in specific empirical cases. For example, in the ownership of basic utilities the state and its citizens may share sovereignty with the corporate board of directors and ultimately with private shareholders. In wartime, or in times demanding emergency conditions, the state may, however, extend its sovereignty and jurisdiction over both private organizations and/or aspects of their functions, e.g., labor unions, defense industries, pension funds, and others. Similarly the question of sovereignty is complicated within what is normally thought of as the private sector, for sovereignty over some seemingly private organizations, such as the YWCA or the local council of community services, may rest not with the "owners" but in members, or community representatives.

Interesting as these mixed or "borderline" cases may be, organizations that represent the sovereignty of the state because they are integral to it (are "owned" by it) are fundamentally different from privately owned organizations in the ways that their goals are set and the ways that they obtain legitimacy. They differ in the processes by which they are controlled and changed.

This leads to the second major distinction between public and private organizations. Public organizations are to a much greater extent dependent for their *financing* upon the public fisc, that is, upon taxes collected by governmental agents and processes. Thus, the immediate recipient of service is usually not the funder. In some cases, such as the post office, the funder *is* the recipient. But, even in the case of the post office, rates are subject to political constraints that are absent in competitive markets.[13] Similarly, when the National Health Service in the United Kingdom decides to charge for prescriptions, the issue is raised—or controlled—on the floor of the House of Commons.

The ultimate funder—that is, the taxpayer—of a public organization's output is usually unable to discern the linkage between his taxes and the benefit accruing to him from specific organizational outputs; the price-utility relationship is lost. Indeed, one of the central functions of government is the making of decisions about "collective" or public goods, those which because of their indivisibility and externalities have effects on everyone, even though individuals could not afford to purchase them or, would wait for others to provide them because of low individual interest.[14]

For instance, clearer air, military defense, space exploration, zoning codes, all have aspects of collective goods that are usually provided by government. Other goods such as general education appear to mix collective and private interests. Although governments provide collective goods, they also make decisions to provide groups or individuals with goods that have no clear relation to concepts of collective goods. In modern times, such private benefits from outputs are often couched in the rhetoric of societal interest. Whether a governmental product is in fact a public good as defined by economists, the taxpayer is only indirectly involved in the decision to purchase it. Moreover, while some of the benefits of a pure "public good" like defense (for example, deterrence of and protection from attack) may accrue to all, the provision of these goods (through defense contracts) has differential impact. Also the value placed upon the benefits or the degree to which the benefits are perceived differ sharply among individuals. Taking differential benefits in defense, for example, "People employed in the missile industry benefit more than those producing bayonets. For militant pacifists it has positive disutility because it appears to them to squander resources in a socially harmful way."[15]

Thus, invariably the imbalance of utility provokes the questioning of a publicly funded organization's legitimacy. As Benjamin Walter puts it, "Politics is an endless game of beggaring Peter to pay Paul. Paul may be happier but Peter (at the very least) grumbles."[16] In the private sector one grumbles and doesn't buy. In the public sector one grumbles and perhaps writes his congressman, supports an interest group, or, at best, votes differently, but only for candidates in general, not for specific outputs. Whatever the action, the market effect is lost.

The emotions engendered by the authority of the state and the constraints placed upon the flow of resources having their origins in tax revenues are among the organizational features that need highlighting in the study of public administration. Figure 1-1, in an oversimplified manner, helps clarify the basic politicoeconomic differences between public and private organizations.

If the distinctions between public and private organizations were sharp and complete, one would say that public administration theory (PAT) concerned itself solely with organizations in Cell A, whereas management and organizational theory would apply to those in Cell C. PAT would pass off, or treat as marginal, organizations falling in Cells B and D as well as C. On the other hand, if the distinction were irrelevant, one would expect to find few significant organizational-administrative differences that are related to the basic distinctions: Organizations located in Cell A would be confronting the same constraints and dilemmas as those in B, C, or D. Clearly this is not the case. Public funding and ownership *do* create relatively distinctive administrative and organizational features. Moreover, a viable and vital public administration cannot restrict itself

Ownership

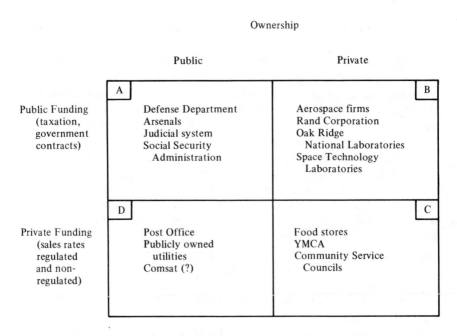

	Public	Private
A		**B**
Public Funding (taxation, government contracts)	Defense Department Arsenals Judicial system Social Security Administration	Aerospace firms Rand Corporation Oak Ridge National Laboratories Space Technology Laboratories
D		**C**
Private Funding (sales rates regulated and non-regulated)	Post Office Publicly owned utilities Comsat (?)	Food stores YMCA Community Service Councils

Figure 1-1. Political and Economic Differences Between Public and Private Organizations

to that narrow domain of state-owned organizations. Therefore, if the student of public administration is to understand the ways in which the state organizes to carry out its policies, he must pay attention to the proliferation of ownership and funding forms in modern societies, to organizations described as "mixed" cells B and D.

Public Administration and Policy Analysis

Public administration deserves separate theoretical development not only because of the organizational differences of agencies due to political and economic characteristics, but because of their crucial role in making and executing public policy. As we have noted, public agencies visibly reward and deprive in the name of society. Of course, private actors have a role in public policy; so political science has diligently studied such nongovernmental actors as interest groups. Nevertheless, our understanding of public policy will be enhanced by the fuller development of a public administration theory that has as its center of concern the public organizations that act in the name of the society,[17] for public agencies carry out and shape policies, and in so doing they contribute to or detract from the effectiveness and legitimacy of regimes.

Therefore, if significant contributions to political science are to be made, policy analysis and public administration of necessity must be thrust into a symbiotic relationship. A theory of *public* administration seems far more likely to provide the advances needed than would a general theory of administration, because it would pay detailed attention to the consequences of organizational structure and process for policy implementation. The abilities, problems, and limits of agencies in carrying out policies is part of the ongoing definition of governmental effectiveness. The independent regulatory agencies, the courts, the various governmental departments are each charged with producing a service or product to implement some public policy. The relative satisfaction-dissatisfaction of citizens, groups, and political officeholders with the manner in which policy is implemented is part of the process by which allegiances and regime support is shaped and effected. And the satisfaction-dissatisfaction balance affects the ability of the regime to mobilize support for other policies and programs.

A theory with the capacity to analyze public organizations as key actors in the policy process would go even further. Public administration must move toward a conceptualization of the American (and other) political systems that (1) recognizes the importance of public administrators as part of a policy-making-and-executing elite;[g] (2) recognizes the importance of institutionalized policy subsystems centered around key public organizations charged with administering policy in a given functional sector (American examples: federal highways, Indian affairs, mine safety, intelligence, oil and gas, tobacco, conscription; non-American examples: oil and gas development in Mexico, cocoa marketing in Ghana, public education in Turkey, etc.);[h] and (3) is able to handle broad-gauge organizational analysis of the key institutional actor in a *policy subsystem*.

Fremont Lyden et al. emphasize the relationship between political science's ability to analyze policy and its ability to perform broad organizational analysis:

---

[g]For an excellent step in this direction see Francis E. Rourke, BUREAUCRACY, POLITICS AND PUBLIC POLICY (Boston: Little, Brown, 1969). Also the reader he edited, BUREAUCRATIC POWER IN NATIONAL POLITICS (Boston: Little, Brown, 1965). Note, we are in no way prescribing that bureaucrats think of themselves as politicians. We are urging analysts to recognize that, norms to the contrary notwithstanding, the bureaucrat is an actor of major importance in a political system. He may think and try to act as an "administrator," but objective analysis can usefully view him as a political actor. At the very least he helps to shape the definition of the situation for political officeholders.

[h]Douglas Cater refers to these as subgovernments—in POWER IN WASHINGTON (New York: Vintage, 1964), pp. 17-20. See also Lee Fritschler, SMOKING AND POLITICS (New York: Appleton-Century-Crofts, 1969); and J. Leiper Freeman, THE POLITICAL PROCESS (New York: Random House, 1965). David Truman also discusses the problem in POLITICS AND GOVERNMENT IN THE UNITED STATES, 2d ed. (New York: Harcourt, Brace & World, 1968), pp. 151-53. By "Institutionalized" we mean the development of well-defined roles and patterned interaction among subsystems' members. The process is akin to that of institutionalization of an organization. See Philip Selznick, LEADERSHIP IN ADMINISTRATION (New York: Harper & Row, 1957).

Construction of a systematic analytic framework [for policy analysis] must begin with an examination of the nature of the organizational entity.[18]

Roger Hilsman also points to the necessity of a public administration that is oriented toward policy process and organizational analysis:

By making it easier for some people to have [more] access than others, by providing for the accumulation of one kind of information and not another, or by following procedures that let some problems rise to the top of the government's agenda before others—in all these ways some organizational arrangements facilitate certain kinds of policy and other organizational arrangements facilitate other kinds of policy.[19]

Organization is also politics in still another guise—which accounts for the passion that men so often bring to procedural and organizational matters.[20]

The political economy framework is the sort of conceptual tool that might guide the development of a PAT oriented toward policy process and focused heavily on organizational analysis. Such a theory might offer some means of bringing analytic order out of the confusion that exists (1) in the myriad of organizational types in the public sector, (2) in determining what is public and what is private, and (3) in understanding the changes that turn a placid environment of a public organization into a battleground. A PAT that could do this would need a central focus on public organizations, for *they* are the discreet phenomena that make up that analytically abstracted entity, public administration. They are, in fact, to public administration what cells are to biology.

In this section we have argued that public administration needs to be a hybrid discipline that has organic links to political science and organizational analysis. The distinctive characteristics of activities in the public sector lie in their relation to state action. Being part of state action affects: citizens' perceptions of the significance of public organizations; basic differences in funding and ownership of public organizations and, therefore, of rights and expectations; and the relationship of such organizations to public policy. These distinctive aspects lead us to see a potential unity and intellectual coherence in the field of public administration. On the one hand, organizations in the public sector are subject to a set of organizational constraints that leads them to respond differently than do other organizations. On the other hand, public organizations are part of policy subsystems that they *e*ffect and that *a*ffect them. Building a theory to explain the role of public administration in the operation of the political system requires a framework that copes with the similarities and differences of public and private organizations.

Intellectual Antecedents[21]

If concepts are needed that can cope with this diversity and with the dynamics of change in the "public" sector, then surely the work done up to now has fallen short. Public administration theories have not met the need, nor has the so-called "organization theory," with which they share a common past and symbiotic present and future.[22]

The studies public administration and organizational sociology had a common link in the schools of scientific management and the thoughts of classical administrative theorists, who developed what were deemed to be correct "principles" of administration.[23] And as the field of organizational sociology developed it drew upon other traditions and, indeed, severed its links with scientific management. In actuality, both Weber's bureaucratic-model, studies of formal and informal organization, and the concerns of the human relations school dominated organization sociology.[i]

Public administration in the meantime has seemed adrift. It was also affected by the development of organizational sociology's bureaucratic model, but limitedly and indirectly. Its classical background too was blasted into ruins, but developments elsewhere, such as discussion of Weber's ideal-type, did not adequately replace it. It was never quite able to shake its normative tendencies; it accepted behavioralism, but did not quite know how to be more behavioral; it did not quite know how to bridge a seeming gulf between the nitty-gritty world of administrative detail and the politics that fascinate most political scientists.

During the decades of the 1930s and 1940s some of the most able minds in political science were drawn toward public administration and wrote on subjects like the "bureaucratic state" and the relation of interest groups to the administrative process. (V.O. Key, Robert Dahl, Pendleton Herring, Avery Leiserson, Charles Hyneman, and many others; all focused their research in this realm.) Considering the times, their ideas were relatively behavioral and nonprescriptive, but their works never became part of the main flow of public administration studies. They were considered more a part of the mother discipline of political science. There remained an apparent gulf between the nuts and bolts of public management, with which public administration seemed stuck, and the politics of bureaucracy, which seemed just as clearly an adjunct of political science.

It became faddish to say that the dichotomy between politics and administration was false. No matter how often the assertion was repeated, however, it did not become clearer just how politics and administration were intertwined. Just exactly how accounting systems, personnel classification systems, or budget categories were tied to politics in any significantly exciting way remained a mystery.

The many public administration textbooks that appeared merely reflected the

---

[i]Chester Barnard stands somewhat apart from the development of both organizational sociology and public administration, though both have drawn upon him. There were few developments this seminal writer did not predate. His work is so far-reaching and insightful that it does not fit neatly into any "school of literature" though most drew from him. It may be that the Barnard had the insights but lacked the scholarly training to develop them or it may be that he is difficult to understand. See FUNCTIONS OF THE EXECUTIVE (Cambridge, Mass.: Harvard University Press, 1938).

field's malaise. To the standard chapters—which once again destroyed the classicists, asserted that politics and administration were one, and descriptively covered planning, personnel, and budgeting—were added ones on behaviorism, bureaucracy, organization theory, and computers. But the old and the new had no cohesive ties, no conceptual linkage.

There was one near-exception to this—the text by Simon, Smithburg, and Thompson. Though intended as a basic textbook it was the closest the field of public administration came to a unified and comprehensive analytical framework for the study of organizational behavior in the public sector.[24] Basic concepts were consistently developed and interrelated, the essentials of a paradigm for scholarly study in any field. Although it had its own subtle normative and paradigmatic problems, it at least eschewed normative prescription of the classical style. And even though it has a distinctive "how to do it" flavor that sometimes gets in the social scientist's way,[25] for all its advances the work of Simon et al. did not serve as a paradigm for public administration.

First there was the stylistic problem: It was written as a basic text and thus filled with general material that obscured the conceptual framework that underlay the work.

Second, though it took a behavioral approach, it represented a shift away from a union of organizational sociology and public administration. As Landau notes, Simon's thought represents a strong shift from organizations as the phenomena to be studied to the interpersonal, interpsychic effects of organizational structure on human behavior.[26] Although most of the critical analysis of Simon's thought has concentrated on works other than the *Public Administration* text, much of it is applicable to the latter. It is Simon's conceptualization of administrative phenomena that permeates the text.

The third feature of Simon, Smithburg, and Thompson that kept it from becoming an adequate paradigm was deep-seated and related to its fundamental level of analysis. It was simply not intended as an analytical device designed to deal with the dimensions or causal relations among variables over the totality of an organization and its setting. It was more likely to spell out dimensions and suggest causal relations on a micro-level of analysis—for example, in dealing with sociopsychological aspects of organizations (morale, loyalty, identification), or in organization control (securing compliance and assuring "right" decisions are made at lower levels). In this sense the work is an *extension* of traditional or classical PAT. It is a modernization or bringing to bear of "real science" upon classical concerns and therefore is neoclassical.

A fourth problem lies in the handling of organizational change. An adequate paradigm requires some explanatory leverage on the processes of agency change, yet Simon, Smithburg, and Thompson, in the tradition of the classical theorists, tend to leave organizational environment and its influence on the agency as an unexplained residue, as an assumed constant or unanalyzed quantity, or treat environment only in terms of survival.[j] Consequently, their treatment of change is casual and unsystematic. For it is in the environment of organizations that the major source of change is to be found, especially in public agencies. And it is environments that play a leading role in the changes that take public organizations from the realm of placid routine to crisis and controversy. To ignore the dynamics of agency-environment relations is to reduce the quest for theory to analysis of administrative (or in the case of Simon, management) techniques, or to an examination of organizations as closed systems.

But the major problem was conceptual. It purposefully sought to avoid any demarcation of public from private administration. Simon, Smithburg, and Thompson were aware of public-private differences but tried to minimize them, saying at one point that "large-scale public and private organizations have more similarities than they have differences."[27] This is probably true at a certain level of analysis but begs the point as to the quality or significance of the differences. For reasons indicated earlier a framework that could become a paradigm capable of unifying focii and advancing an empirical theory of public administration must center on those qualitatively different aspects of *public* administration. This the work of Simon and his colleagues failed to do. What Dwight Waldo says of Simon's work in general holds true of the text as well:

Business Administration, by virtue of its greater commitment to efficiency and its narrower range of . . . what shall I call it? . . . value-concern, found Simon more meaningful and acceptable than did Public Administration, which just at this moment in its history was breaking down the barrier between "politics" and "administration," admitting and emphasizing the relevance of administrative means to social, economic and political ends.[28]

We could be accused of criticizing Simon, Smithburg, and Thompson for not developing a paradigm when that was not their intention. But this is not our aim. (Our criticism helps to highlight the requisites of an adequate framework.) It is very much to their credit that a book intended as a textbook nearly fulfilled the role of a paradigm for theory building.

The impact of Simon, Smithburg, and Thompson on organizational sociology was quite marginal, but there were further advances in that field that pre- and postdated the publication of their book. Because the political economy framework draws upon those advances, it is important to note them. During the last two decades a fairly extensive literature that treats complex organizations as social systems has developed. This literature has broken from, and gone beyond, the earlier contributions of literature in the traditions of scientific management, human relations, and Weberian bureaucracy. The literature of complex organizations treats organizations as dynamic, adapting, internally differentiated systems. Where human relations research emphasized group cohesion, morale and attitudes of personnel, research on complex organizations or, as it is sometimes

---

jThe closest they come to treating organization environment is in Chapters 18 and 19. It is an excellent treatment but one that focuses on survival threats from the environment rather than one that sees the environment as a steady source of influence to change or not change—constraint and/or opportunity.

called, "organizational analysis," focuses on organization survival, effectiveness, and adaptation. Unlike much of the earlier work, the literature on complex organization has not been concerned with showing how informal structure departs from the formal; instead it has treated both as outputs of system processes. It has avoided focusing on bureaucratic characteristics and their pathologies. And, finally, it has eschewed the search for a singular model of organization structure and process—a search which was the trademark of the scientific management approach.[k]

Organizational analysis has attempted to be nonnormative. When it does state prescriptions for organization effectiveness, it has suggested the contingent conditions under which the prescriptions might be most effective.[29] It is essentially a structural functional approach. As such it treats the *full* range of social system processes—recruitment and socialization of personnel, authority, and control patterns, conflict and tension resolution, role conflict, goal adaptation, management processes, technology of tasks accomplishment, and adaptation to environment as ongoing processes of an interacting social system.[l] The political economy approach seeks to capitalize upon the advances made by writers in the field of complex organizations—particularly the focusing on the organization as an equilibrating social system with external and internal dynamics.

Key Dimensions of Political Economy Analysis

According to Kuhn a paradigm should create "a research tradition," it should focus the efforts of students upon key dimensions or aspects of a phenomenon. The proposed framework for the study of public administration would accentuate the place and role of public organizations in policy subsystems and two key

---

[k]It should be said that the early literature of complex organizations has, like public administration, suffered from the lack of a paradigm. Dwight Waldo referring to the fable of several blind men attempting to describe an elephant says: "In view of the inclusiveness, the diversity, the amorphousness of the materials put under the organization theory heading nowadays, one must conclude that if they all concern the same elephant, it is a very large elephant with a generalized elephantiasis." Dwight Waldo, "Organization Theory: An Elephantine Problem," PUBLIC ADMINISTRATION REVIEW 21 no. 4 (Autumn, 1961): 216. The later literature has more focus.

[l]Although structural functional analysis has been criticized for its focal emphasis on equilibrium and stability functions, its alleged fault has existed more in the mind of the critics than in reality. See Rolf Dahrendorf, "Out of Utopia: Toward a Reorientation of Sociological Analysis," AMERICAN JOURNAL OF SOCIOLOGY 64; as Flanegan and Fogelman point out, most political scientists who have used the approach have applied it to the study of profound change. See "Functionalism in the Social Sciences," American Academy of Advanced and Social Science, Monograph 5 (Philadelphia, 1965), p. 119. In fact it can be argued that the approach handles change quite well. See Charles P. Loomis, "In Praise of Conflict and Its Resolution," AMERICAN SOCIOLOGICAL REVIEW 32, no. 6 (December 1967): 875-90.

aspects of organizations—their political and economic structures and processes. The interpretative literature about organizations that has been produced by analysts of complex organizations has been rather fragmented and diffuse. Each analyst has presented a case, or set of cases, showing that the greatest heuristic and analytic leverage lies in goals, communications, raw materials and technology, socialization, and so on. Some of this disparity may ease as more comparative studies are done, but the problem lies deeper than the case approach. Rather it is the lack of a widely accepted, yet sharply focused framework in approaching the subject. The diffuse, social system approach does not focus on the most important variables accounting for structures and change.

Our fundamental assumption is that, just as the social systems we call "nation-states" vary in their political economies—their structure of rule (or succession to high office), of power and authority distribution (their division of labors, incentive systems and modes of allocation of resources)—so, too, do the social systems called "public organizations."

The phrase "political economy" has a long history and several meanings. At one point it implied a relationship of government to economy so as to promote a competitive marketplace. This was a normative definition; for political economy maximized, through the invisible hand of the marketplace and the profit motive, the efficient allocation of resources and the production of goods and services. Modern welfare economics also uses the phrase in a normative sense. To oversimplify, welfare economics seeks that policy alternative which benefits the most people with the least cost. In this sense economy refers to efficiency, to minimization of cost. In the late 1960s a concern for PPBS (Planning-Programing-Budgeting-Systems) and cost-benefit analysis transformed what had been a theoretic discipline into a practical tool for analyzing concrete policy options.

But it is also possible to use the phrase in a descriptive way. We define "political economy" as the interrelation between a political system (a structure of rule) and an economy (a system for producing and exchanging goods and services). Any description must examine the component systems, the polity and the economy, as well as their points of intersection.

In general, analysis of political systems has two major components: (1) ethos, or values, and (2) power system. That is, "political" encompasses both power and the values (ends) which power is used to achieve.

An economy is a system for producing goods and services. A description of an economy consists of two parts: (1) a statement of the goods and services produced, their quantities, and through which organizational forms they were produced; and (2) a definition of the mechanisms, rules, and institutions that shape *exchange* of goods and services.

A general comment is in order about the difficulty of drawing a sharp line between political and economic phenomena. Shifting for a moment to the polity and economy of the United States, it is clear that an individual's, group's, or institution's position in the economy can be used to effect the structure of rule. The accumulation of wealth from efficient production of goods or services can be used to effect the policy choices of government and even the structure of government itself. Moreover, individual choices of buyers and sellers aggregate to effect policy options. If individual buyers purchase many Volkswagens, they not only effect our balance of payments, they effect United States policy options and hurt domestic automobile manufacturers. The auto industry may in turn push for a change in laws and legislation. Similarly, the political system uses power to shape the economy: both the rules under which it operates and the goods it is to produce. President Nixon's 1971 freeze on wages and prices is only the most conspicuous example. Thus political and economic systems inevitably interpenetrate. It is this very interpenetration of the two systems at the level of organizations that gives our framework its heuristic, analytic power, its ability to synthesize diverse studies. But the interpenetration leads to some ambiguity as to when a given action is political or economic.

How can the approach of political-economic analysis, originally applied to nations or societies, be used at the organizational level? Throughout this essay the terms "political" and "economic" when applied to organizations will be used in the following ways:

Political connotes (refers to) matters of legitimacy and distribution of power as they affect: the propriety of an agency's existence; its functional niche (in society, political systems, and/or policy subsystems); its collective institutional goals; the goals of the dominant elite faction; major parameters of economy, and in some instances its means of task accomplishment (if the task is vague enough to effect values or if values change sufficiently to bring established means into question).

Political scientists often make the mistake of defining politics and the political in terms of contentiousness and conflict. Many things that are often noncontentious are relevant to understanding the political system—two examples are political socialization and habits of compliance. Moreover, an agency with stable and legitimate goals has a political regime, a distribution of authority, and institutionalized goals as much as does a system in conflict. The basic point is that politics refers to the structure and process of the uses of authority and power to affect definitions of goals, directions, and major parameters of the organizational economy.

If a given organizational goal could be implemented through one and only economy (technology or means), then the choosing of that goal would dictate the corresponding economy. But several different organizational economies might achieve the same primary goal. Thus the organizational elite may choose among several alternative economy or technology structures according to their political values. The dominant political values will probably reflect a preference of the elite for other goals to be achieved along with the primary one. A housing program in a socialist country or a new civil rights program is set up in such a way as to minimize political dissent as well as to accomplish the respective prime goals of more housing or equal opportunities. Thus the selection of an economic structure that achieves the primary goal and satisfies others as well can be a complex and difficult *political* matter.

It is important to note the last point in the above connotative definition. Even tasks performed by lower functionaries (e.g., claims examiners, investigators, project officers, policemen, intelligence operatives) can become political if values extant in the environment or within the organization are affected by the discretion granted persons at lower levels. Or it may be that the task is vaguely defined; and consequently performance defines values. Yet another instance of "means" becoming political may occur when a long-established and accepted mode of task accomplishment affects values and legitimacy owing to changes occurring in the parameters of values held within and without an organization.

Economic connotes (refers to) the combination of factors of production, the arrangement of the division of labor, allocation of resources for task accomplishment, and maximization of efficiency. [m]

An organization's economy is its system for producing the "output" of the organization, it is the combination of men, money, machines, and facilities to produce "desired" output. Where goals are well established and means routinized, the economy operates like a well-ordered machine, and organizations become administered devices.

Also encompassed within its economy are the various factors that affect the cost of producing a given output, maintaining a given level of service, and the cost of delivering the same. For example, the Strategic Air Command or the Department of Defense (depending on which level of analysis one is engaged), have a distinctive cost curve with regard to delivering the output of "deterring enemy nuclear attack." Given the population and area of the United States a high cost must be incurred to obtain any deterrence at all; after that, given increments of deterrence (say reducing probability of attack from 1 in 5 to 1 in 100) can be obtained by relatively smaller expenditures; and finally the cost of maintaining a given level of deterrence decreases unless or until some externality such as a change in weapons balance occurs, at which point the costs would again sharply increase.[30]

---

[m]More than a few economists will be unhappy with our connotative definition. Modern analytic economics tends to focus on maximization and resource allocation. Our definition includes these but also focuses on the structure of the economic system, the extent and limits of differentiation, and coordination to accomplish tasks (produce goods and services). The question of choice, which is paramount to microeconomics, is one of many concerns to us.

Factors such as the above, commonly treated as economic by economists, easily verge into the political realm when considering public organizations. Because so many other actors influence its ability to obtain resources and factors of production, the high cost to SAC of replacing its aging B-52 manned bombers may easily become a political matter involving the legitimacy and indeed the very survival of the organization; thus, the question of cost becomes a question of policy priorities and values. Despite the blurring of lines, definite analytical pay-offs result from considering at some point the economy of a public organization. We consider the threshold between economy and polity to be crossed when cost factors become questions of legitimacy and organizational direction.

An organization's political-economy can be analytically divided into internal and external (environmental) aspects. Figure 1-2 below summarizes *some* of the key features of an internal and external political economy. The *external political*

Figure 1-2. Major Components of Political Economy for

Typical Public Organizations

	Environment structure and process	Internal structure and process
P O L I T I C A L	*Superordinate and authoritative executive bodies and offices (and organized extensions–budget, personnel offices) *Superordinate and authoritative legislative bodies and committees (and organized extensions–ombudsman, inspectorates) *Independent review bodies–courts, judiciary *Competitors for jurisdiction and functions *Interest groups and political parties *Media-communications entrepreneurs *Interested and potentially interested citizenry	*Institutionalized distribution of authority and power Dominant coalition or faction Opposition factions, etc. *Succession system for executive personnel *Recruitment and socialization system for executive cadre *Constitution Ethos, myths, norms, and values reflecting institutional purpose *Patterns for aggregation and pressing demands for change by lower personnel
E C O N O M I C	*Input characteristics: labor, material, technology, facilities, supply and cost factors *Output characteristics: demand characteristics and channels for registering demand *Industry structure (in and out of government) *Macro-economic effects on supply-demand characteristics	*Allocation rules Accounting and information systems *Task and technology related unit differentiation *Incentive system Pay, promotion, tenure, and fringes *Authority structure for task accomplishment *Buffering technological or task core

aspects of organizations consists of exchanges between external actors (individuals, groups, or institutions) and a public organization for control over legitimation, resource base, goal definitions, and the channels for exertion of influence. As implied earlier, one of the relatively distinctive features of public organizations is the greater degree to which external actors are directly involved in setting goals, allocating resources, and granting or withholding legitimacy from them. Crucial to the understanding of external political environment would be analysis of the power and rights of allies, hostiles, and competitors.[n] Political scientists have done a good job of describing the political environment of public organizations and the ability of such organizations to manipulate as well as react to it.[31]

Analysis of the economic *environment* of agencies deals with the supply and price schedules and behavior necessary in obtaining factors of production and the exchange of output at organization boundaries, assuming or holding constant organizational and program legitimacy. It deals with what in the private sector is referred to as "industry structure" and its relationship to distinctive features of technology, the supply of raw materials, and the labor market structure. It has not been customary to subject public organizations to this type of analysis, probably because they have been presumed to be not only sole providers of a particular service or product but also passive recipients of price and technology. But it does not follow that an agency is not affected by or has no discretion over matters in its economic environment.[o]

The internal polity refers to that part of the internal structure of authority control, and influence relating to broad questions of survival, institutional goals, dominant elite goals, major parameters of economy, and legitimacy of function. Internal polity encompasses these aspects of internal authority structure whether that structure is formal or informal, constitutional—representing established and dominant values—or anticonstitutional—thus challenging those values.[32]

Classical theory, of course, relied heavily on tables of organization to describe formal authority relations. Later, analysts emphasized informal organizational authority patterns. But the internal polity is more complex than both of these. Analysis of polities must encompass the following: the building and maintenance of organization cadre; the dominant coalition or faction within it, their views of what the institutional goals should be, and those who might be opposed; the reliance on external support by the dominant or challenging faction, and

---

[n]By competitors we mean other organizations directly competing for function, jurisdiction, or resources. These we treat as political, not economic, because they are identifiable and have aggregated resources.

[o]If our framework focused solely on *internal* political-economy the phrase "political-administrative," or "political-managerial" model might more easily connote our concerns; but it doesn't. It is imperative that we also describe the economic *environment* of public agencies. Furthermore, the political-economy framework can be applied to social movement organizations, churches, and other less clearly "managed" organizations; and in such instances the term "administration" connotes too much rationality to be applicable.

succession patterns for top leadership; the relevant values in key groups essential to task accomplishment; cohesion among lower level personnel; distribution of power among department heads of similar formal rank; and the influence of organization constitution. Any of these things when viewed as part of internal polity are seen in the role of contributing to the primary polity function: the translation of original mandate into operative goals and programs.

The internal economy involves to some degree patterns of authority, but only those that can be sorted out analytically as clearly adapted to task accomplishment. It involves what has traditionally been called "managerial" or "administrative authority." Where a technology is well fixed, for instance, supervisors and middle-level personnel have authority arising from the need to coordinate positions and to control quantity and quality of production. Central to the internal economy of an organization are the way its tasks are accomplished. Considerations are available technologies, incentive structures, coordination and communication spans, areal dispersion, and labor-capital intensity ratios. *Public* organizations, like private ones, differ in their men-machine mixes, routinization of tasks, visibility of performance to cadre and external actors, sheer size, and geographic dispersion. Analysis of the internal economy focuses on the ways in which the factors of production are combined to produce an output or product, assuming a given definition of goals and policy directions. It focuses upon organizational means, rather than upon definition of goals.

Conclusion

This chapter has reviewed the quest for a theory of public administration and for parallel and related events in organizational sociology. Our orientation leads us to urge pursuit of a theory of public administration that is empirical, oriented toward public policy and policy subsystems, and focused upon analysis of public organizations that are key actors in a policy subsystem. This can be done through a framework that, by synthesizing the conceptual direction of past work, sharpens and highlights the operation of the organizational social systems.

The political-economy framework highlights the interaction of internal and external structures and processes. To illustrate, a change in the economy of courts and penal institutions occurs in the form of an increase in the forced supply of "raw material" to be processed, e.g., criminals arrested creates organizational problems for courts and prisons. External political actors (e.g., newspaper editors, officeholders, social movement groups) criticize the courts and prisons. Judges, lawyers, prison officials react, and so on. A change in any one sector creates opportunities and problems for actors in other sectors. The political-economy framework is intended to synthesize not only previous research but disparate subfields as well. For instance public finance and accounts have not been treated as behavioral subjects; they have been seen as technical (even how-to-do-it) subjects. For us they are treated at least in part as critical elements in organizational behavior that have political and economic consequences and causes.

In the chapters that follow we draw heavily upon American experiences to illustrate the various dimensions of the political-economy framework. Yet it should be clear that we believe the framework to have applicability across time and cultures. We attempt to show this at least briefly in the concluding chapter.

2
The Environments of Agencies

Traditional and neoclassical (Simon et al.) writings in public administration have tended to treat both the external political and the external economic as givens, as matters beyond the scope of PAT. For us they are central. Any organization exists in an environment made up of users and suppliers and of interested and disinterested others. Furthermore, it exists in a society that provides definitions of appropriate means to be used to reach specific ends. A public organization may be mandated to provide services to individual citizens, who then become part of the immediate-in-contact environment, e.g., the postal service or the Veterans' Administration. Or it may be mandated to provide service to, or control of, other public units, e.g., the Office of Management and the Budget vis-à-vis the Department of Commerce and other "line" agencies. In the latter instance the agencies-in-contact become part of one another's immediate environment.

A dynamic analysis must focus upon environments of organizations because it is there that many of the major pressures for change occur. Clientele may inundate the organization, making it impossible for the organization to meet its goals. Or an organization's goals may be unexpectedly and drastically altered by a sovereign executive. Both these calamities befell the Office of Emergency Planning in 1971 when President Nixon suddenly ordered it to enforce a wage and price freeze. Another example occurred in the late 1960s and early 1970s, when courts and jails in many states were overwhelmed with petitioners and prisoners[a] as a result of rising crime rates and liberal Supreme Court decisions, leading to massive delays in the settling of cases.

A private business can often regulate excess demand and strain on capacity by raising prices or by rationing output. Many public agencies are required by law to provide their services to process all claimants. Where "demand" is excessive both the quality and level of service may seriously deteriorate, leading to a clamor for new resources for the organization, reform of its procedure or structures, or even transfer of its function to other agencies.

Significant others may press for changes in the definition of organizational

---

[a]Analytically, there is some question as to whether business and other forced clientele (cases that the public agency is required to process) should be considered as clientele or as the "raw material" that interest groups (clientele), funding agencies, and sovereigns require the agency to process and handle. Because cases and prisoners must be processed the productive task of many agencies is the processing of claims and people, for they are the raw material that is acted upon (shaped) by the organization. As long as one is aware of how the term "clientele" or "raw material" is being used, the distinction should not be troublesome.

mission. For example, antiwar groups and the Senate Foreign Relations Committee pressed for redefinition of American military posture and activity by the Departments of State and Defense, and the presidency.

What is needed is a set of analytic concepts and variables for describing and interpreting environments. Exactly how are demands transmitted? What are the analytic concepts and related variables that explain differences between organizations, or that, changing over time, affect the administrative choices of organizational cadre and the executive cadre of an organization?

As noted earlier, the environments of organizations can usefully be divided into economic and political structures and processes. Within these broad rubrics, interactions and exchanges can be isolated. But organizations are also affected over time in the wider society by events which funnel into a particular agency's political economy. Before analyzing the external political economy of public organizations it will be helpful to discuss more general features of the environments of public organizations.

Sentiment Distributions and Environmental Dynamics

A public organization is part of a policy subsystem, an arena of individuals, groups, and organizations, of "relevant others" affected by and interested in a given policy.[b] The relevant others have a role to play or an interest in influencing an area of policy for which a particular public organization has prime concern. These relevant others represent a variety of actors in and out of government; interest groups, competing public organizations, superior organizations, individuals, appropriation subcommittees, subject matter committees, and staff agencies. They may be competitive, cooperative, hostile, overseeing, reviewing, controlling, but regardless of their role they shape the mandate and the conditions of existence for a public organization.

Relevant others differ in the amount of influence or resources they can bring to bear on an organization and their readiness to do so. Some individuals or groups have little interest in an organization. For our purposes they are "irrelevant" others. Other individuals may have an interest, but do not have resources that they can readily mobilize. For instance, an individual veteran dissatisfied with his treatment at a VA hospital will not be able to affect VA policy or service unless dissatisfaction is widespread among other veterans and they are able to mobilize political support.

[b]Douglas Cater, POWER IN WASHINGTON (New York: Vintage, 1964), pp. 26-48; David Truman, POLITICS AND GOVERNMENT IN THE UNITED STATES, 2d ed. (New York: Harcourt, Brace & World, 1968), pp. 437-78. Or, see J. Leiper Freeman, THE POLITICAL PROCESS: EXECUTIVE BUREAU-LEGISLATIVE COMMITTEE RELATIONS (New York: Random House, 1965), p. 22. As we use the term "relevant others," it refers to those individuals, institutions, organizations, and groups that are perceived by the organizational cadre to be relevant to them and the organization by dint of their interest in its output or input and latent or manifest ability to influence it.

By way of contrast, some groups or individuals may have resources that they can use to influence policy but for a variety of reasons fail to exercise it. For instance, superordinate offices in cabinet departments may fail to review and control their subordinate bureaus because of limited attention span. Or they may fail to review and control because of the political costs of being too involved (e.g., the President vis-à-vis the "Plans" division of the CIA).[c] To the extent that recipients or suppliers of service to public organizations are organized but unable to concert on specific policy issues because of internal conflicts or differing orientations, they may be unable to bring their resources to bear on a public agencies and its policies.

Both the powerless individual and relevant others who have resources to influence agencies but do not use them (low-contact-influentials) affect agencies in a tonal or background way. Executive cadres may be more or less attuned to their preferences. Especially if they have great potential for influence, the executive cadre will be inclined, at least in a negative way, to recognize these preferences. That is, they will avoid taking steps that would arouse the interests of the latently powerful.

By and large, agency executives have to be most concerned about those directly related or in-contact groups and individuals who have resources to influence the agency (the in-contact-influentials) and are willing to use them. These may be interest groups like the United Mine Workers, Chile's Fedicameras, the Committee of the American Steamship Lines, Argentina's Rural Society (SRA), the Veterans of Foreign Wars, and the Farm Bureau Federation that are in regular contact with a public organization; or they may be other public organizations competing, opposing, wielding authority or exerting influence upon the organization in question.[d] These public organizations may play a role in aggregating the resources and interests of others and bringing them directly to bear upon an organization.

An actor that is weak from the point of view of one agency may be seen as strong or highly influential by other agencies or actors. For example, a smalltown newspaper may be unimportant to an agency but very important to a congressman sitting on that agency's appropriations subcommittee.

The environments of public organizations vary widely in the consensus-legitimacy patterns that characterize them and in the breadth and intensity of opposition or support to the agency, its goals and programs. Or put another way, agencies environments vary with the precariousness of the values their means and ends represent.[1] The shape of such patterns depends on the dramaturgy or emotive element in the public organization's operations; the perceived expertise

---

[c]"Plans" or "DDP" (Deputy Director for Plans) of the CIA is the coyly contrived name for covert political operations, the so-called "dirty tricks divisions" of the CIA.

[d]Fedicameras is a peak association of commercial and banking interests in Chile. The SRA is the venerable and powerful Argentine equivalent of the American Farm Bureau Federation. We are indebted to Riordan Roett of Vanderbilt University for this and other examples of public organizations in Latin America.

of the organization; the degree to which its impact is perceived; the breadth (number of groups and individuals affected or interested) of its relevant others; the intensity (perceived value) of their interest; and the resources they can bring to bear in influencing the organization.[2]

The Bureau of Narcotics and Dangerous Drugs, the Selective Service system, the Soviet Ministry of Agriculture, the New York subway system, the Security and Exchange Commission, the Brazilian Superintendency for Economic Development of the Northeast (SUDENE), and the Welfare Department in Plaquemines Parish, Louisiana, all face environments with different patterns of breadth and intensity that change with time and circumstance. The subway system reaches tens of thousands, but intensity is low except in case of accidents, fare increases, or a rush of muggings. Moreover, clients are not generally organized. The welfare department in the poverty-stricken parish of "Boss" Leander Perez must deal with only a few relevant others (Perez and henchmen), but their resources and control are overwhelming.[e]

Figure 2-1 seeks to provide an example of relevant others for the Selective Service system as of 1967, and to indicate by placement on the chart the influence they had on Selective Service. The chart is organized as a solar system: the closer to the center the more powerful the actor or group. It also separates relevant others into allies and hostiles. Where an actor is closer to the vertical line it means that as of 1967 he was neutral or unknown in his support or opposition to the status quo for Selective Service.

Some public organizations find at given points in time that no one has a deep interest or commitment to their outputs or technology. Accordingly, they are vulnerable to "imperialistic" expansion by competitors or to the vagaries of economy drives. the United States Information Agency and the Agency for International Development face apathy toward their goals and occasionally hostility toward their technology. The Bureau of International Organization Affairs of the State Department, Brazil's Administrative Department of the Public Service (DASP)[f] California Board of Pilots for the Bays of San Francisco, San Pablo, and Suisun find scant support for output or even for their existence.

In other circumstances, public organizations (such as the Bureau of Prisons, Brazil's National Indian Foundation FUNAI, Job Corps, California Board of Psychiatric Technicians)[g] find that some of the relevant others who could

---

[e]"Racist Leader," TIME, 12 December 1970, p. 2. Perez runs the parish (county) with an iron hand, does everything he can to keep blacks from obtaining welfare, and threatens troublemakers with imprisonment in a snake-infested concentration camp.

[f]DASP is the hapless organization established to carry out the establishment of a merit civil service system, but because of the importance of nepotism and political connections in access to positions, the Brazilian political system provides a rather unsympathetic environment for it.

[g]The California Board of Psychiatric Technicians would make a fascinating case study in futility. Established to regulate the type of persons licensed to work as attendants in mental hospitals, it was afraid to impose anything but the lowest standards for fear they would make it impossible to find anyone for these difficult jobs at terribly low pay. The board

Figure 2-1. The Environment of the Selective Service System

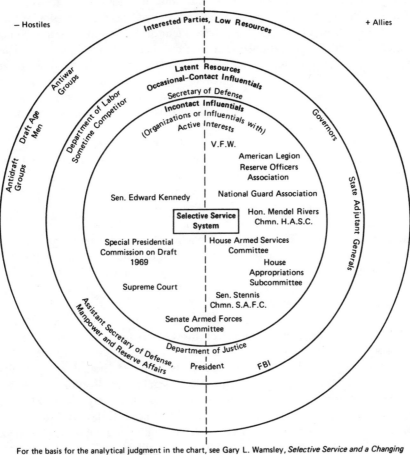

For the basis for the analytical judgment in the chart, see Gary L. Wamsley, *Selective Service and a Changing America* (Columbus, O.: Charles E. Merrill Co., 1969), *passim*.

provide positive support lack the resources and ability to mobilize or exert influence, or that the relevant others wish to hold it to a status quo, with which the organization is less than satisfied.

Precariousness of organization values often grows out of intense and polarized

wished to lobby within government for higher wages, but was afraid to raise license fees to obtain the permanent staff necessary for lobbying for fear there would be an outcry, resignations, or a drop in recruits. No interest, no efficacy, no resources, no results.

FUNAI was set up to protect and promote the welfare of Brazilian Indians after years of cruel exploitation and scandals. It receives more lip service than substantive support. Its position was quite similar to the United States Bureau of Indian Affairs until recently.

sentiment distribution among their relevant others, e.g., the National Labor Relations Board in its early years.[3] In some instances precariousness results from relevant others with intense interest but limited breadth and distribution. California Board of Guide Dogs for the Blind, United States Commission of Fine Arts, and the Alaska Railroad of the Department of the Interior have intense but limited support. Others experience intense but limited opposition. The unique features of the public sector make it difficult to predict the fortunes of an organization with intense but limited-interest patterns unless one carefully analyzes the extent to which support or opposition has managed to influence key in-contact others for the organization, such as its appropriations subcommittees.

Still other public organizations have solid and widespread support among mass publics for the values their outputs and processes represent. This combined with strategically influential elite support makes their environments benign. For example, in the 1950s the Strategic Air Command basked in the warmth of a widely held value, defense against a Communist threat, and enjoyed support from local interests near its bases, well-placed congressmen, and defense-contractor interest groups. The Bureau of Public Roads operating on a highway trust fund to build the highly popular interstate highway system has led an idyllic life for a number of years now. Other examples might include the FBI, the CIA, the British National Health Service, Venezuela's Central Office of Coordination and Planning (CORDITLAN),[h] the United States Weather Bureau, and NASA.

Figure 2-2 reflects our guesses about the variations in the breadth and direction of sentiment distributions of the general public and of influential in-contacts for a variety of agencies and programs. It should be clear that distributions have to be combined with analysis of the strength of particular hostiles or allies in order to predict the relative stability or directions of possible change of an organization or program. An agency can have only a narrow base of support, but if its supporters are all powerful, it needs little else. Indeed, one might define an "unresponsive institution" (a common complaint in modern America) as one in which large segments of the general public or of in-contact others desire change, but where the most powerful relevant others are unwilling or unable to use resources to change the agency in question or its policies. The example of the NKVD, the Russian secret police during the time of Josef Stalin, is intended to indicate how in some instances if key influentials support an agency it can even dominate both a hostile public and other elites. The death of the dictator immediately changed the base of support of the agency.

In discussing the distribution of sentiment in an organization's environment, note must be taken of its fluidity. Most organizations strive for at least a bland and benign environment, but in fact may move from one extreme to the other.

---

[h]CORDITLAN is the bipartisan supported planning agency established to use Venezuela's petroleum revenues in a "rational" way and in a way "above politics." Accorded this type of status it has had an invulnerable and inviolate position.

Figure 2-2. Hypothetical Depiction of Sentiment Distribution Among
General Public and In-contact Others

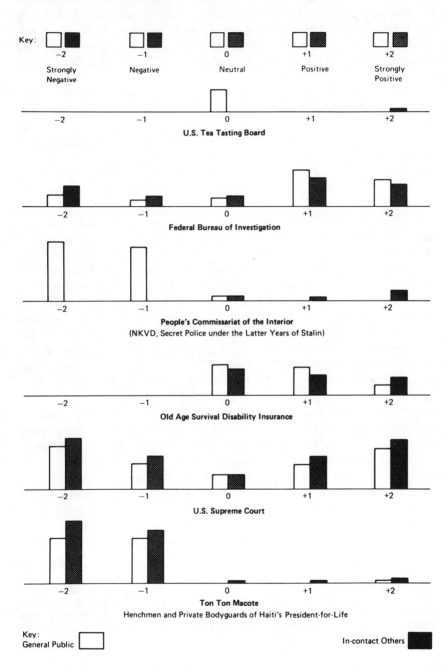

Since they purportedly act in the name of society as a whole, symbolize the coercive power of the state, and draw funds from the public treasury, public organizations are often involved in a struggle to secure the precarious values their processes and products represent. Generally, they are successful in achieving placid or benign environments, but few are ever completely secure. Sentiment distributions vary in their (1) malleability to which an agency may with some success apply its efforts and (2) changeability, to which it must largely adapt itself.

As David Truman argues, administrators try to make the controversial routine by obtaining an equilibrium of interests.[4] But Truman also notes that despite this persistent drive, the equilibrium can be upset by administrative error, changes in influence patterns, and technology.[5] Or some latently powerful actor may suddenly turn attention upon an agency as a result of some happenstance. For instance, in 1970 the United States Tea Tasting Board was "discovered" and proposed for abolition because it seemed to be a dispensable governmental function.[i]

Until recently the Post Office operated in an apparently placid environment. No one seemed to have strong preferences or feelings about it except at Christmastime. It met an apparently depoliticized need with its cost buried in the general taxes. Economists, management consultants, and politicians recognized its inefficiencies and inequities and had made proposals for its reorganization, but they were never politically viable. An unexpected glut of mail and packages in Chicago and a postman's strike in New York in 1970 brought extraordinary pressures to bear upon it, leading finally to its reorganization as a government corporation. Abrupt changes in the equilibrium of interests can be seen in many agency profiles: the Subversive Activities Control Board, when a presidential appointment smacking of cronyism received publicity;[j] the CIA, after the Bay of Pigs incident; Brazil's Petrobras (government oil monopoly), with the appointment of a leftist general to head it in the 1950s; and the Bureau of Indian Affairs, after Native Americans began to develop militancy and public figures such as Jane Fonda began to denounce the bureau.

Whether or not impinging environmental phenomena grow out of an environment's malleability or changeability, most public organizations manage to achieve relative placidity. The capacity of public organizations to benignly institutionalize their policy subsystems and to smooth out turbulence is quite remarkable. Negative effects are often alleviated by developing support among key in-contact others. A good example is the Selective Service system, which

---

[i]The tea distributors proposed to pay the costs of operating it themselves, because it provided them a necessary function: it regulated the quality of tea in America.

[j]The Subversive Activities Control Board was found to have done virtually nothing for years. Some minor tempest like the appointment of a White House secretary's husband touched off a row. Brazil's controversial Vargas regime brought Petrobras into the political wars by appointing to head it a man who began to claim that it could serve as a model for nationalizing many other industries.

between 1965 and 1969 used the House and Senate Armed Services committees, the American Legion, the V.F.W., the National Guard Association, and other military interest groups to stave off an immense amount of sustained pressure from Congress, the courts, and a presidential commission.[6]

Even though a public organization can manipulate its environment and external influentials might attempt to change that organization, major change may be very difficult to achieve, because it, as compared to a private organization, is more dependent on others for the definition of its goals and procedures, an agency, even if it perceives a need for change, depends largely on others to define that need, and these "others" usually view any given public organization as only one among several interests that can be given only partial attention.

More importantly, goals and procedures may be frozen by the conditional pattern of support and hostility to the organization. A press for change mobilizes opposition. The incentive system of public organization also militates against organizational cadres pressing for change. A political actor seeking a change in goals or operations must generate issues, mobilize a coalition of forces, and gain the support of key proximal others in a policy subsystem.[7] Such changes occur infrequently. In fact it has become part of the "conventional wisdom" of American statecraft that it is easier to establish a new organization to accomplish a task than it is to change an old one to accomplish it.

Political scientists who have concerned themselves with the "politics of bureaucracy" have tended to focus on the periods of turbulence that surround the open struggle to bring about change in public organizations. But understanding of organizational change might be greater if we were to study the processes of change before they surface in the bureaucratic politics struggle.

To date, students have generally failed to identify and study the sources and processes of change at earlier points. It may be possible to identify potentialities for change and its points of inception. The patterns of sentiment among relevant others (and change in them) must be analyzed as they are filtered through and shape an organization's political-economic exchanges. Empathetic analysis of the actors in a policy subsystem can help identify their self-interest and thus their behavior and its role in change. Shifts in internal polity or seemingly unintended consequences of internal economic changes must be seen as sources of change that can affect an entire organization. The political-economy framework seeks to alert the analyst to look for the sources of change in the interconnections between all four analytical sectors.

External Political Structure and Patterns of Interaction

An external political structure reflects a distribution of sentiment and of power or power resources among directly involved relevant others (in and out of government). The sentiment distribution, which affects the specific adaptative and manipulative strategies of agencies, must be weighted by the power and coalitional interdependencies of these relevant others.

Distribution of Power Resources

It is obvious that among such diverse agencies as the United States Tea Tasting Board, the Department of Defense, the NKVD, the Conseil d'Etat in France, or a central planning agency in Brazil, there are different ranges of intensity and breadth of support-opposition in the general public and among relevant others, who, in turn, have different degrees of influence or resources. Discussion of sentiment distributions surrounding agencies must be linked to a discussion of control over power resources. In the United States Congress a committee chairman is more powerful than a committee member because he holds certain power resources. Under the rules, he controls when a committee meets and when it votes. If he does not like what he thinks it will decide, he may not let the committee vote. One chairman may be more powerful than another, because a wide range of other committees are dependent upon action by the one he chairs (e.g., the House Ways and Means Committee or the House Rules Committee). Outside of government, one interest group association may be more powerful than another. An association of bankers is more powerful in influencing a state banking department than an association of psychiatric technicians who have low pay, status, education, and poor organization.

The differing patterns of external support and the agency's stance vis-à-vis its environment can be seen in the records of testimony before congressional subcommittees. For example, Ira Sharkansky analyzed the content of official records of budget-hearings testimony before the Fogarty subcommittee of the House Appropriations Committee.[8] The study focused upon the budget strategies of four agencies—the Office of Education, the Food and Drug Administration, the Children's Bureau, and Howard University. Table 2-1, adapted from Sharkansky's article, depicts his summary of a quantitative content analysis of the agencies' support before the Appropriations subcommittee.

It is apparent that the Office of Education received the greatest political support from the incumbent administration (1959-1963), and from other sources. Although Sharkansky's data covered only four years, there is reason to believe these were relatively stable patterns throughout the post-World-War-II era. The large differences in levels of external support for the agencies is striking and some were able to sharply increase their budgets with this support. Table 2-2 indicates these budget increases.

Although Sharkansky's work focuses upon the amount of positive external political support, it is well however, to remember that agencies may be surrounded by hostiles as well as allies. Each agency has a complex pattern of

Table 2-1
External Political Support of Four Agencies

	Office of Education	Children's Bureau	Food and Drug Administration	Howard University
(1) Number of groups testifying	1	2	3	4
(2) Breadth of Interest of Testifying Groups	1	2	3	4
(3) Nonsubcommittee congressmen testifying	1	2.5	2.5	4
(4) Support by President and staff				
(a) lines in presidential budget message	1	3	3	3
(b) lines in secretary's statement	1	2	3	4
(c) generosity of superior budget offices	2	1	3.5	3.5

Source: Sharkansky, "Four Agencies and an Appropriation Subcommittee: A Comparative Study of Budget Strategies," *Midwest Journal of Political Science* 9, no. 3 (August 1965): 273. Numbers are assigned values; 1 is highest, 4 lowest.

supporters and opponents. Theodore Lowi has developed a typology of public policy arenas (or subsystems) based upon patterns of consensus-conflict, group alignment, and breadth and intensity of their involvement.[k]

Three major *domestic* policy arenas or types are discussed in the typology: distributive, regulatory, and redistributive. Different programs and agencies can be classified into one of these types. *Distributive arenas* are those in which there is general consensus on the social value of implementing certain policies or programs benefiting specific groups, organizations, or communities. The key characteristic of the distributive policy arena is the fact that the wide consensus on the output of the program and the disaggregation of benefits to a large number of recipients makes it difficult to realize that Paul's benefit both

[k]Theodore J. Lowi, "American Business, Public Policy, Case Studies and Political Theory," WORLD POLITICS 16 (July 1964): 677-715. Also "Distribution, Regulation, Redistribution: The Functions of Government," in PUBLIC POLICIES AND THEIR POLITICS, ed. Randall B. Ripley (New York: W.W. Norton, 1966), pp. 27-46. See also Daniel Willick, "Political Goals and the Structure of Government Bureaus," paper delivered at American Sociological Association, Washington, D.C., 1970.

In a personal communication Lowi has argued that it is the written law which structures the policy arena. To the contrary we assert that it is the consensus-conflict patterns that structure the law, and that it is changes in these patterns that change the law. We do not disagree with Lowi that once the law is enacted its formal provisions have a powerful effect upon the patterns of claims and pressures upon agencies. The law structures both the polity and the economy of an agency.

Table 2-2
Percentage Increase in Budget Requests 1951-1963

Office of Education	Food and Drug Administration	Children's Bureau	Howard University
2,120	565	335	280

Source: Sharkansky, "Four Agencies and an Appropriations Subcommittee: A Comparative Study of Budget Strategies," *Midwest Journal of Political Science* 9, no. 3 (August 1965): 257.

excludes Peter's benefit *and* imposes cost on Peter. This is often true of public policies, but it is least obvious for distributive policies. It should also be noted that a particular policy may be perceived differently at different points in time. Thus social security programs for unemployment and retirement benefits may have been once viewed as redistributive at the outset, but now may be viewed as distributive.

The public organization with prime responsibility for a distributive policy takes a fixed amount of funds, or value, and divides them among clientele groups (existing or potential). But the decisions distributing benefits can be fairly easily routinized, bureaucratized, and made to appear the result of "objective criteria." The fact that Paul may be benefiting more than Peter is successfully downplayed and misperceived. The prevalent perception is that anyone can be a Peter under certain circumstances. The door to the benefits is open to all if they are in certain circumstances or meet certain "objective" criteria. Corps of Engineers river projects, or highway- and bridge-building decisions of the Bureau of Public Roads, Social Security, veterans benefits, Agricultural Extension Service, all are either distributive programs or agencies at the center of distributive policy arenas.

In such an arena the primary agency is likely to have a fairly stable and quiet environment. There may be conflict, but it is relatively low-key, behind-the-scenes, and according to certain well-defined rules and procedures, including log-rolling.

Regulatory arenas are those in which the statutes as passed reflected an intention to control an industry or sector of society. Control of routes and rates for railroad and airlines, and allocation of radio and television station franchises are examples of regulatory arenas. The policies as originally formulated are specific and individual in their impact. Clearly someone would benefit and someone else would be deprived unless the policies were somehow altered in their implementation. The regulatory agency with primary responsibility starts with a much different environment than does one in the distributive arena. The agency armed with only an assigned concern for a vaguely defined public interest faces intense and efficacious groups bent on protecting their interests against the "highhandedness of the state." Although great efforts are usually made to

Table 2-3[a]
The Arenas of Power

Policy Arena	Primary Political Units	Relation Among Units	Power Structure
Distributive	Individual firm, corporation	Log-Rolling, mutual noninterference, uncommon interests	Nonconflictive elite with support groups
Regulatory	Group	"The Coalition"; shared interest on subject matter; bargaining	Pluralism; multicentered; "theory of balance"
Redistributive	Association	The "peak association"; class, ideology	Conflictual elite, elite, and counterelite

[a]Theodore J. Lowi, "Distribution, Regulation, Redistribution: The Function of Government," p. 39 in *Public Policies and Their Politics*, ed. Randall B. Ripley (New York: W.W. Norton, 1966).

technicize and bureaucratize decisions, the lower level of societal consensus and the contentiousness of the regulated make these efforts always something less than successful. Conflict is between interest groups and regulatory agencies or between one set of claimants and another. And yet, while channeled through hearings and legal proceedings, conflict is still intense with bargaining, threats, coalition-formation, sanctions, and so on. Finally, things can reach a stage of relative quiescence if the regulating agency becomes virtually the puppet of the groups it is meant to control. In that case the analytic construction of "regulatory arena" becomes rather meaningless, perhaps replaced by a "self-regulatory arena."

Redistributive arenas are those in which quite clearly Peter is being taxed for the benefit of, or at the expense of, Paul. Broad categories of citizens are affected and the status and economic standing of one group in relation to another are seen as being effected or potentially affected by the policies. As Lowi says, "expectations about what it *can* be, what it threatens to be, are determinative."[9] Tax rates on different groups, some types of welfare programs, unemployment insurance, public housing, and Office of Economic Opportunity programs may be examples. Conflict is likely to be intense but broad with "peak associations," classes, and parties involved in the struggle. The breadth of the issues involved places conflict in the center of political debate, in the legislative arena.

Lowi's students have demonstrated that the typology has predictive value.

For instance, L. John Roos has shown that distributive bills are essentially passed as recommended by their sponsoring committee while redistributive bills tend to be amended on the floor. In these latter cases the range of interest and lower consensus prohibit a committee consensus.[10]

Where Roos has shown that the external political structure varies by arena, Daniel Willick's study of sixty-two United States governmental agencies indicates that the internal task structure of agencies also varies by arenas. For instance, among other things, he finds that the percentage of clerical workers is higher in redistributive agencies than in the others. Lowi's theory predicts this because external conflict and breadth of effect lead redistributive agencies to have very specific rules and procedures.[11]

Although Lowi's tripartite typology is disarmingly simple,[1] for present purposes its importance is twofold: First it links aspects of the external political structure to the internal political and economic structures of agencies. The technical skills and characteristics of agency personnel, the amount of discretion they have, the internal span of control are all related to the nature of fundamental agency tasks. Second, and more immediately relevant, it helps us understand the diversity of agency environments. The external political structure and relations effects and shapes the ongoing adaptations of agencies to their environment.

Interaction and Adaptation

The reader may grant that agencies differ in their external political patterns, but what determines how an agency adapts to that pattern? Why are some agencies

---

[1]Lowi's categories of regulatory, distributive, and redistributive arenas actually represent complex combinations of several variables (consensus-conflict, breadth and intensity of interests, divisibility of output, and so on). Moreover, agencies providing predominant group consumption or *collective* outputs (the Department of State, the Department of Defense, or, on a local level, the Fire Department) are ignored. The biggest problem one encounters in stretching his ideas in the direction we have, i.e., from classification of statutes to classification of policy subsystems, is that his concepts do not deal with change over a period of time: for example, a change from regulative arena to a self-regulative, or the change of the progressive income tax from a redistributive policy to virtually a distributive one by the erosion of its progressive base. These changes may not reflect changes in the "power structure" of the American political system, which is the level at which Lowi and others have been debating, so much as they represent incremental changes among the participants in a policy subsystem—while some have their attention diverted and others find their power resources spent, and so on. Just as the power resources of international politics differ in their utility in general war as opposed to insurgent warfare, so do the power resouces of organizations and groups differ in their efficacy from one situation to another. The power resources so potent in getting legislation passed (a general war?) may be less useful in the long twilight struggle over the implementation and administration of policy (guerrilla war?).

One other important change over time that may result in a need to reclassify a policy and its arena is the general change in attitudes of both interrelated groups and the mass public. Social Security may have had a radical ring to it at one time, but it now barely stirs a ripple.

assertive and aggressive and others quiescent? What determines the short-run changes in agency posture?

External political interactions grow out of the more or less institutionalized patterns of power and influence that surround an agency. External political exchanges stem (1) from the conscious efforts of external actors to affect the organization's functional or niche goals, or the goals of the executive cadre, and/or to affect its major economic parameters by altering its resources or its legitimacy; (2) from efforts of a public organization to manipulate its relevant others in order to maintain or increase its legitimacy and resources, thereby sustaining or changing its goals and overall direction. Specific external political interactions and maneuvers affect a public organization's niche,[m] its functional goals, its internal political pattern, its processes of task accomplishment (insofar as they involve questions of legitimacy), and even its survival.

Most public organizations have some capacity to manipulate their environment—neutralizing some actors and making allies or protectors of others. A public organization engages in power struggles over its niche or domain. According to Levine and White the domain of an organization consists of (1) goals it wishes to pursue in the future—these represent claims on future functions it is trying to stake out, and claims on the requisite resources to perform the functions, and (2) present functions being carried out—these represent *de facto* claims to these functions and the resources to effectuate them.[12] Thus executive cadres of public organizations are most often seeking to alter their agencies' domain or that of their "neighbors." They may do so to alleviate their uncertainty about key parts of their own domains or merely to establish firm control of it. These drives for certainty and control are strong because a prerequisite for a public organization's continued existence is external support.

When we think of the external political interactions and pressures between an organization and its environment we tend to think of the obvious: For instance, the coming to office of the Nixon administration in 1968 is said to have brought a different set of pressures to bear upon the Civil Rights Division of Justice and the Office of Civil Rights of the Department of Health, Education, and Welfare. The President and high-level political executives evidently endeavored to subtly shift these organizations from zealous pursuit of desegregation in the South to a more diverse, lower-key nationwide approach. The new approach would not hurt the growth of Republicanism in the South and might, in fact, even enhance it. It was said to have been done not merely through explicit instructions but also by

---

[m]The concept of niche is borrowed from ecological studies of biotic communities. Each organism exists in an interdependent symbiotic web, each species adapted to climatic and environmental conditions and to one another in such a manner that it can simultaneously survive and contribute to the survival of others. Similar but nonbiological is the concept of "domain." See Sol Levine and Paul White, "Exchange as a Conceptual Framework for the Study of Interorganizational Relationships," ADMINISTRATIVE SCIENCE QUARTERLY 5 (March 1957): 444-63. We will use the two interchangeably for stylistic relief.

a conscious refusal to give the positive political cues necessary for vigorous enforcement of civil rights laws, and by creating ambiguity and uncertainty, and thus developing a belief among subordinates that they would receive a negative or null response to any enforcement efforts requiring positive political support.[13] But this is only the obvious; external political exchanges are varied and complex, and public organizations vary widely in their sensitivity to political impingements and in their ability to manipulate or ameliorate their environment.

Several factors contribute to variation in sensitivity and manipulative capacity.[n] Among these are the degree of goal ambiguity or clarity; the extent and/or ease of surveillance by actors in superior positions; the extent to which an organization's services satisfy central societal values as compared with peripheral or precarious ones; the structure of funding and executive personnel appointments; the structure of institutionalized support (in-contact influentials, sporadic-contact influentials, irrelevant others, intense but narrow interests), and the ability to serve supporters so as to obtain concordant feedback.

Goal Ambiguity or Clarity. Where goals and even processes are clearly defined (assuming they are subject to surveillance) some public organizations have little room for maneuvering or for choice. They are locked into a well-defined mold by statutes and the review of superiors. For example, the Social Security Administration or the Tennessee Department of Employment have little opportunity for entrepreneurial maneuver or changes in orientation. Their environments are depoliticized to a large extent, there is little hostile scrutiny, and program means and ends are specified. Their growth is tied to population increases, cost of living changes, and occasional statutory changes like Medicare (affecting Social Security). Thus these agencies are left with almost no chance to deviate in goals, in program ends, and or in processes.

However, where goals and values are ambiguous or multiple, a public organization's elite may press for one definition or another and, within the boundary of political feasibility, may allocate some resources internally in pursuit of their choice. Examples might include a state college (teacher training or regional university center), the Smithsonian Institution (collector of the nation's memorabilia or educator and cultural force), correctional institutions for delinquents (treatment or custody), the Federal Reserve Board (economic growth or monetary stability), or state departments of parks and recreation (preservation or utilization).

Surveillance. Some public organizations effectively avoid scrutiny by external actors. The CIA with its budget hidden in other departments' appropriations is the most notable example of an agency largely shielded from scrutiny. But even when a public organization's budget is subject to review, the surveillance may be

---

[n]Sensitivity (the awareness of environmental pressures and constraints) may vary independently of an agency's ability to manipulate its environment.

ineffective because of ambiguity of goals; hidden missions; or simply the overwhelming complexity of programs and accounting information.

For example, the University of California (like many state universities) possesses most of the characteristics that thwart surveillance. Goals could scarcely be more ambiguous, and the complexity of multiple sources of funding and immense capital-outlay projects of long and varied duration make surveillance a massive task, challenging the capabilities of budget agencies or chief executive. Where the tasks of a public organization are difficult to scrutinize, control passes inward to its executive cadre, and sensitivity diminishes.[o]

Centrality of Values. If a public organization is perceived to be effectively realizing a central value of the political culture, it is likely to be left with more autonomy (at least of means). In fact it will probably be left with considerable power to manipulate its relevant others and "write its own ticket" regarding resources and legitimacy. This blissful state has its limits, however, and no public organization experiences it indefinitely.

If it is seen as charged with achieving a central value but is perceived ineffective, it is likely to come under intensive surveillance and its environment politicized. An example might be the office of the State Fire Marshal charged with ensuring fire safety in schools, institutions, and public buildings. As long as there are no tragic fires the office is left with a great deal of autonomy. But a single fire traceable to ineffective enforcement can result in a severe loss of autonomy and minute surveillance by relevant others. A state police agency that suffers a revelation of corruption may face a similar fate.

Personnel and Funding Allocation. The sensitivity and manipulative capacities of a public organization are partly a function of the degree to which its personnel and funds are contingent upon behavior of external actors. It would be a mistake to assume that all public organizations are equally dependent on external and superior actors. Some develop special, strategically placed allies that can help or hurt them in terms of financial resources. For example, in the 1960s the National Institutes of Health and the Department of Health, Education, and Welfare were careful to inform Congressman Wilbur Mills, chairman of the House Ways and Means Committee, of any major changes in medical programs, and, in some instances, to obtain his approval of the changes.

---

[o]Governor Reagan's struggle with the University of California affirms rather than counters this point. Reagan has been able to make his desires felt, but considering the effort expended, the university by and large still fits Franklin Delano Roosevelt's depiction of the Navy department as a "feather bed." "You punch with your right and you punch with your left until you are finally exhausted, and then you find the damn bed just as it was before you started punching." Arthur Schlesinger, A THOUSAND DAYS (Boston: Houghton-Mifflin, 1965), p. 406.

Public organizations that operate on users fees, trust funds,[P] or special funds derived from license fees or special taxes may enjoy a greater freedom from surveillance by superiors than those operating on general funds. They also tend to have low sensitivity to any interests but those of their special clientele. Clientele which pay special fees and taxes to support a public organization tend to view both it and its funds in a proprietary manner, subject solely to their scrutiny. Such surveillance as the organization in question experiences is likely to come from its special-involved relevant others, which may make it virtually a captive. These special, in-contact influentials—e.g., an appropriations subcommittee, an interest group or a budget agency, some of which are in control of its resources—may come to hold the real influence over an agency rather than the agency's formal superiors doing so. The organization may thus be relatively autonomous of formal superiors, but a prisoner of those it is supposed to serve or regulate.[q]

For example, the retail liquor industry of California decided it wanted a "fair price law" to sustain retail prices and prevent price cutting by large discount houses. Its interest groups had the appropriate legislation introduced, lined up crucial committee support, and informed the governor and budget division that they were willing to have "their" taxes increased and "their" money spent to augment enforcement staff of the Department of Alcoholic Beverage Control. The industry received all that it "asked" for.[14] Other examples of funding structures that enhance an agency's autonomy from formal superiors abound at state levels.

The channels for appointment and terms of office of personnel also affect the relative autonomy of agencies. Compared to private organizations, public agencies' relative lack of control over appointments of executive personnel is a major constraint on direction and goal choice. (Of course, external control or intervention extends down to lower-level personnel as well. Budget offices usually have "position control" over personnel, and sometimes central personnel agencies share this power.) The nature of executive appointments may be partially decided by the very groups the organization is supposed to control or regulate.

But the nature and extent of this control by external actors varies widely among agencies. As a general hypothesis, the longer the terms of appointments of executive personnel, the less the vulnerability to external political impinge-

---

[P]The autonomy that might be expected to accompany a public organization's financing from trust funds is often offset by a very clear and singular goal: for example, a state employee's retirement system or the United States Railroad Retirement Board. They are thus insulated but dependent. They cannot redefine their goals, but have considerable autonomy in executing their tasks within sharply defined limits. At the same time they are relatively impervious to outside intervention.

[q]The Bureau of Public Roads and the American Road Builders Association and the American Association of State Highway Officials; the California Department of Alcoholic Beverage Control and the liquor industry.

ments. That Federal Reserve Board members are appointed for fourteen-year overlapping terms is surely a factor in the board's autonomy, and one that has caused several presidents to gnash their teeth. Those public organizations headed by boards or commissions with overlapping terms are somewhat insulated from political impingements, even though they might be financed from general revenues (FCC, ICC, SEC, etc.). It takes major external threats to agency survival and long-range, massive shifts in the sentiments of relevant in-contact others as well as of its own executives to change the directions of these commissions.

Some public organizations at the state level may operate from general funds, but the fact that their chief executives are elected gives them a strong base for autonomy. The California attorney general is elected (sometimes by a greater margin than any other official) and the Department of Justice that he heads thus enjoys relative freedom from interference by interest groups, the governor, the budget division, and appropriations subcommittees. (Of course it also pursues central values and ambiguous goals.) Although the legislature formally controls appropriations for such offices and bureaus, election gives their executives a mandate and autonomy—that other agencies may not have—from both the legislature and the governor's office.

The Structure of Support and an Established Feedback Loop. Beyond the factors listed above, an agency gains external support if it offers a well-received product to an efficacious clientele; a clientele able to influence key, proximal others so as to enlarge the organization's share of resources and legitimacy.

Aaron Wildavsky offers numerous examples of public organizations struggling to achieve such a feedback circuit and thus provide for security and expansion. For instance, the United States Census Bureau did housing surveys of such diffuse interest that appropriations subcommittee members failed to be enthusiastic despite support from a few national interests such as Armstrong Cork and the building materials industry. But when the bureau also initiated *local* surveys useful to area interest groups, committee members fortified with localistic demands became supportive.[15]

The delicate balance needed for an effective feedback circuit is revealed in such cases. Interest-group power is often equated with a national membership base such as possessed by the building materials industry. But given the local base of Congress and the nature of the appropriations process, the Census Bureau's output and feedback were too diffuse and the industry's support insufficient. The bureau needed a specific, locally based output and feedback that would create zealous advocates in some strategic points of its policy subsystem.[r]

---

[r]One of the Selective Service system's major strengths has been its presence in every county in America. See Wamsley, SELECTIVE SERVICE AND A CHANGING AMERICA: A STUDY OF ORGANIZATIONAL-ENVIRONMENTAL RELATIONSHIPS (Columbus, O.: Chas. E. Merrill, 1969), pp. 70-71.

An effort to move in the opposite direction of the Census Bureau and develop a well-balanced output and feedback circuit can be seen in the Soil Conservation Service's switching from a few large-watershed projects concentrated in a limited geographical area to many smaller projects spread throughout the country. The service successfully broadened and diversified its base and thus increased its capacity to ameliorate and influence its environment. Similarly the Grazing Service merged with the Bureau of Land Management to diversify its support beyond the confining embrace of the stockmen and their organizations.[16]

In addition to manipulating and maneuvering for a more advantageous distribution of allies, public organizations foster and create their interest-group support. The Soil Conservation Service did much to foster the Association of Soil Conservation Districts, which now provides the mainstay of its support.[17] Among the best-known examples of the ability to develop and foster interest-group support are the various military services: the air force, the Air Force Association; the navy, the Navy League; the army, the Association of the Army. The services also receive support from a host of associations representing various defense industries and the various veterans groups. Before campuses became so politicized, the military services saw ROTC as more than just a source of manpower; they also saw it as a means of forging close supportive bonds between civil and military elites. And until the National Rifle Association became noisily involved in the struggle over gun control legislation it received large quantities of supplies arms and ammunition from the military. Indeed, the army still finds it worthwhile to maintain good relations with the National Guard and its related group, the National Guard Association.

David Truman has pointed to other means available to public organizations in their efforts to manipulate or influence environment: (1) the establishment of advisory committees; (2) the formal inclusion of interest groups in administrative structure; and (3) propaganda aimed at relevant others and mass public.[18]

Summary

External political interactions take place between a public organization and its relevant others at its boundary. The transactions may involve its output, work, product, and/or inputs of resources and legitimation. We treat inputs or outputs as political rather than as economic when they are of sufficient magnitude to alter niche, overall goals, direction, and major economic parameters. A public organization's output may be material (parity prices, contracts awarded, services rendered) or it may be nonmaterial (status, prestige, recognition); it may also be deprivation or sanction, rather than reward.

External political events can be short-run in effect; for instance an agency's budget may be held down for a year or two because it made some tactical error in the struggle over appropriations or in dealing with groups and institutions with whom it has aligned itself; or they can be long-run in effect; when a change in external political sentiments change the valuation of an agency's output.

Some political exchanges are intended to produce results that are more symbolic than substantive. The establishment of a draft lottery in 1970 in response to widespread discontent was treated by the Nixon administration and the Selective Service as a major reform, but in fact it may have been a means of preserving the Selective Service system in an unaltered form for the time being.[19] Its aim may have been maximizing political quiescence at minimum political cost.

Pressures may arise largely from key in-contact others—for example, Wilbur Mills and his influence upon HEW's Health Services and Mental Health Administration; the late Mendel Rivers' influence upon Selective Service or the armed forces; or Congressman John Rooney's impact upon the State Department.[20] Other pressures originate with groups which are not directly in contact and whose influence is aggregated and brought to bear through a key other like an appropriations subcommittee. Apparently this was the case with the Soil Conservation Service.[s]

Pressure may arise also from indirect and diffuse sources but in such intensity and volume that it by-passes benign actors that usually buffer an organization. Such seems to have been the case for the Food and Drug Administration when it was hit by the thalidomide panic in 1962. The agency and its procedures for drug testing were brought under heavy attack for permitting public sampling of a foetus-deforming drug. Its allies were powerless to protect it from the deluge of criticism, although the long-run impact on the agency remains a subject for debate.[t]

An organization's relevant others endeavor to affect its resources and the legitimacy of its existence and/or enterprise; their ability to do so depends upon a variety of factors and conditions which reflect its vulnerability or imperviousness.

Finally it should be reiterated that organizations do not merely react to external political impingments; the phenomenon that occurs is best described as an *exchange*. Public organizations also manipulate, ameliorate, and influence their environment and relevant others. They attempt to effect the overall external political structure as well as specific transactions.

---

[s]The reference is to the case of the service diversifying its projects so as to have a broader-based feedback and support. See Wildavsky, THE POLITICS OF THE BUDGETARY PROCESS (Boston: Little, Brown, 1964), p. 66.

[t]See James S. Turner, THE CHEMICAL FEAST (New York: Grossman, 1970), pp. 217-34. According to Ralph Nader's 1969 task force the agency remains fundamentally unchanged, although procedures for approving drugs may have been altered some as a result of the thalidomide scare.

Economic Environments and Exchanges

Examination of an organization's external economic relations requires an analysis of "industry structure," "markets" structure, elasticity of supply, factors of production, and demand for output. In examining "industry structure" for *private* organizations, attention is paid to the degree of industry concentration, the relationships among competitors, peculiarities of technology and raw materials supply, and factors affecting the distribution network for organizational products. Because *public* organizations are thought of as monopolies, "industry structure" has often seemed to be unimportant. Yet many public organizations do have direct economic competitors. The Post Office competes with the Railway Express Agency, United Parcel Service, and Greyhound Bus for the delivery of small packages, and COMSAT competes with telephone utilities. Furthermore, the "industry structure" of such quasi-public organizations as aerospace firms is obviously of key importance in understanding problems of public administration.

It is also clear that the supply of the factors of production for public organizations is directly affected by events in the economy at large. Comparative wage rates and the ability to attract personnel keep them tied to the general economy.

A major point to be made in discussing the economic environment of public organizations is that many phenomena which might be treated as economic in a consideration of private organizations must be treated as at least partly political. Many of the environmental exchanges of a private organization can be conceptualized as economic—a result of market choices by buyers and sellers—whereas many of those of public organizations, because of their symbolic importance and public funding, and because their demands are aggregated, filtered, and channeled through the budget process and their policy subsystem, are political. This is perhaps more obvious and often noted in the United States because the separation of legislative and executive bodies and the weak party system expose budgetary processes that are hidden elsewhere. But the same phenomena are found elsewhere. In most instances a discreet demand upon an organization that might conceivably be treated as economic at the outset becomes political (1) as the budget process intersects its policy subsystem, (2) as questions concerning the legitimacy of spending public funds for its particular purpose are raised, or (3) as its resource needs are thrown into competition with other public organizations.[u]

---

[u]One cannot say that organizations in the private sector never have the legitimacy of their resource allocation or the nature of their output challenged; the difference between public and private is again a matter of degree. A "private" hospital that has many babies die, has its legitimacy questioned. Where an institution delivers key values it is apt to be taken out of the private realm and put under at least some public control.

Politicizing Effect of the Budget Process. Particularly in the American political system the budget process forces demands through a gauntlet of interest groups, legislative committees, executives, budget agencies, and functional and allocational competitors. Resource levels are seldom a direct and simple function of an organization-environment exchange and of the organization's output competing among infinite products for infinite buyers. Instead, resource levels emerge from a more intense matrix where a small number of actors evaluate priorities among comparatively few organizations, on the basis of their products and the importance of their clientele. The actors in the process are guided by their perceptions of the "political climate," tradition, roles, the desires of certain powerful actors, priorities and trade-offs, and the over-all resource picture. (As noted earlier, some public organizations with a trust fund or user's-fee base or with powerful strategic allies may be more insulated from the particular sets of events that occur in this matrix.)[21]

By compressing a complicated decision process into a rigid time frame, budgeting further distorts the original demand. Jesse Burkhead has described a budget as "the product of a time sequence of decisions made in an organizational context."[22] These pressures have some unusual, and decidedly political rather than economic results—budget deficit crises with all-night filibusters, legislatures "locked-in" by their leadership to secure budget passage, fist fights on the floors of legislatures, governors publicly offering to cut back their budget along general lines but privately threatening to cut back specifically on projects benefiting districts of his opponents. Under pressure of time one may even find, as Anton reports of one budget in Illinois, that "final decisions were made by two men in the governor's private bathroom on the night before the legislative session ended."[v]

Thus the original demands made upon a public organization might logically dictate an extended pursuit of goals on a long-time horizon. The annual or biennial appropriations process may, however, enable enemies and rivals to subvert or redirect its goals by carefully timed strategic cuts in the budget. A public organization may start out upon the basis of a popular social movement or political ground-swell but later may find itself thwarted by a coalition of rivals and competitors who attack it at some particularly vulnerable point in the high-pressure budget process. The Voting Rights Act of 1965 permitted federal district courts to send examiners in to investigate charges of obstructing voter registration. But despite the language of the law, southern congressmen on

[v]The references to political outcomes are taken from Thomas J. Anton, THE POLITICS OF STATE EXPENDITURE IN ILLINOIS (Urbana: University of Illinois Press, 1963), p. 2 and from Wamsley's participant observation in California when the Speaker of the Assembly locked up that body until the economy-minded opposition agreed to pass out the Governor's budget. This they did only after a threat to cut out all the benefits to the opposition. These sorts of events are unusual and dramatic but the so-called normal behavior is just as political even though it may be less spectacular.

appropriation subcommittees tried to block the necessary resources for enforcement.

The lack of a "normal" economic exchange with a public organization's environment results in the absence of market controls with built-in incentives to efficiency. This leads, supposedly in an effort to obtain efficiency, to elaborate accounting and budgetary controls, contract clearance, position control, control of category transfers, competitive bidding, apportionments, cost-benefit analysis, and program-performance-budgeting systems, all of which may develop their own political pathologies.[23] (Note that when private organizations undergo change in their legitimacy and their degree of "privateness," one result may be a requirement that they change their accounting and reporting procedures. The laws and regulations of both the Social Security Administration and the Securities and Exchange Commission has led to publicization of previously private behavior.)

In the public sector rules of accounting often become bones of political contention. A public organization may want to undertake new programs that require expansion of physical facilities, but because capital improvements are under close scrutiny by a central budget office or because the organizational cadre fears they will stir up allocational rivals,[24] they may have their budget request and organizational accounting treat the costs of expansion as "maintenance and repair." Another organization may merely seek renovation of its facilities but find the cost would be $55,000, which under existing accounting rules automatically classifies it as a "capital improvement" rather than as "maintenance and repair," ($50,000 being the breaking point). Accordingly, the organization seeks an exemption from the rule and an intrapolicy subsystem struggle ensues.

There are many examples of accounting and budgeting procedures becoming "political." A change in accounting rules that permits the California Department of Justice to charge other agencies for legal advice given over the telephone sets off a battle within the executive branch of government; organizations providing services at cost to other public organizations feel their very survival may depend on securing the right to include depreciation costs in their charges to users. Public organizations use all the latitude they can find in deciding to which account to charge expenditures, thereby manipulating accounts so as to control the kind of information submitted to reviewers (keeping some expenditures low and running others up to justify increases), or they shift between accounts so as to remain within the "basic budget" and avoid seeking a "supplemental" budget; state organizations with multiple sources of funding (state, federal, special, and general) juggle expenditures from one fund to another, charging expenditures initially to federal funds and later moving incrementally to a state fund base.[25] In each of these cases accounting rules and budgetary matters may have both economic and political ramifications.

The cost curves of producing and delivering of one public organization's product or service differ considerably from those of another public organization. For example, public health costs in eliminating and controlling insect borne disease rise steeply at first but then fall off. More resources are required to reach a certain level of performance than are needed to maintain it afterward.[26] Other products and services decrease in per capita cost but hold the total cost constant as the number of recipients of the service increases up to a certain capacity limit; nuclear deterrence is an example. In contrast medical care, housing, and education increase in total cost as each unit cost possibly holds constant. These internal economic characteristics[w] can, and often do, have external political consequences. The heavy and steep costs of putting in a new weapons system for deterrence or damage limitation (like the antiballistic missile system) may trigger a debate over national priorities, the true nature of risks from attack, etc. Political crises over school costs, however, in at least some geographical areas, may be slow to develop because increasing costs develop gradually and inexorably, rather than appear in "lumps," and are often considered inevitable. Economic characteristics, however, of public agencies do often have such political aspects.

Economic Input and Output

What then is treated as strictly an external economic exchange for a public organization? External economic exchanges at a public organization's boundary are inputs and outputs that neither are intended to nor actually affect niche, function, order of magnitude of resources or major economic parameters; rather they are designed merely to implement established goals and tasks. They are exchanges seen as legitimate, as a normal part of accomplishing tasks, by the dominant coalition, and, if it exists, by an internal opposing coalition or relevant others. Because government is often a major purchaser of a type of product (e.g., autos, typewriters), it is at times in a position to bargain over price and quality, but it often does so without conscious effort to manipulate its environment politically; in yet other instances it must accept the prices set by a market.

The literature of public administration often neglects to deal with economic considerations on such a theoretical basis. Occasionally political scientists assume the successful implementation of a policy is due to public and personal enthusiasms, but the degree of political momentum behind any program is

---

[w]We treat the production function of the organization, cost curves for producing output, as an aspect of the internal economy. The cost of each separate factor of production is largely determined outside of the organization, but their combination is a result of organizational choice in the face of available technologies, mandated services, and political requisites. Since the theory of the firm in micro-economics has been largely bodiless, it has not had to develop a sharp distinction between the internal economy and the economic environment of the firm.

seldom great enough to nullify resource considerations.[x] In fact programs are usually forestalled, curtailed, altered, initiated, expanded, or accelerated because of external economic conditions. Indeed, the internal economy, (modes of task accomplishment), may also be altered in order to adapt to economic conditions; for example, economic conditions may dictate purchase of certain types of raw materials over others with those chosen requiring different handling techniques.

"Raw Materials" and "Products" of Agency. The field of public administration has also left this matter to others because it has failed to conceptualize public organizations as obtaining raw materials from an economic environment and processing or converting them into products offered to consumers.[27] We need to broaden our concept of raw material, product, and product demand. Public organizations often get their product demand from other agencies. Even public organizations with an *interface* role and with, we assume, highly charged political environments have established some niche security and carry on some "production" that no longer raises questions of legitimacy: The Joint Chiefs of Staff during the late 1950s and early 1960s produced the following "products" that we often failed to conceptualize as products:

1. Replies to the National Security Council's request for information and advice on formation of the Basic National Security Policy.

2. Replies to request from the Joint Staff (JCS's work organization) for guidance in preparation of strategic plans and approval of final drafts.

3. Decisions in response to self-generated demands for decisions (or definition of stalemate) on weapon systems and force level priorities.

4. Endorsements in response to requests from the president for support for the Department of Defense budget before the National Security Council or Congress.

5. Advice on military tactics upon requests from political leaders as a result of an unforeseen foreign policy situation; resolution of jurisdictional disputes among the Services or a definition of them for the secretary's signature.

6. A translation of a policy decision by political leaders into general strategic orders for the unified and specified commands.

7. Testimony before Congress.

8. Approvals or vetoes of organizational structures and operational plans of the unified and specified commands.

The demand for these outputs was met by collecting and collating information and beliefs (the raw materials). Internally information and beliefs were processed through technologies of debate; compromise; defined disagreement; suppression of the source of raw materials: or delays in processing raw

---

[x]Moreover the assumption that public "policy" is ever definitely "decided" by a legislative body or any other institution is itself rather meaningless. See Lindblom, THE POLICY MAKING PROCESS (Englewood Cliffs, N.J.: Prentice-Hall, 1968).

materials. The final product was affected by agreement among the Joint Chiefs not to disagree or oppose one another's aims and requests and by their perception of advice they knew was desired. Since they were officially responsible to the administration their endorsement and testimony was technically within the bounds of loyalty to the administration, while offering informal cues of protest. Many of these products of the JCS resemble those of a private consulting firm, but we seldom conceptualize a public organization's products in this way.[y]

Since the JCS had established a functional niche for itself, much of this conversion process no longer raised questions of legitimacy that we would treat as political.[z] Advice to the Joint Staff on plans, translation of policy into strategic orders, approval of structures and plans of unified and specified commands were relatively routine and economic compared to some of the other raw materials described above which tended to be volatile and political.[28]

Another example of a public organization and its products and raw materials may be found in the Office of Management and Budget and state budget offices. They have been affected by changes in the nature of the products they are offering their "customers." The nature of budgeting changed as the product demanded by the chief executives' changed.[aa] The needs of chief executives went from merely controlling expenditures approved by the legislature, to full-scale planning and programing. Thus, they needed a different output from their budgeting offices. Had chief executives fired budget directors with one set of skills or consciously sought to replace them with others and to alter goals and directions of budget offices this would have to be seen as a political impingement on budget offices. However, this was seldom the case. Over the years budget offices slowly began to recruit people with different skills, in response to

---

[y]It must be admitted, however, that the raw materials and techniques of the JCS are by its *interface* nature more threatening to its legitimacy, i.e., more political, than they are for many public organizations.

[z]It should be noted that the JCS operate in a highly competitive situation. They are one of several possible policy inputs in the national-security policy process. Their legitimacy, indeed their existence, depends on their products being accepted once in a while. But their organizational life is complicated by the fact that they must not only act as a "consulting firm" but also as a "coalition of normally competing consulting firms." Each member (except the chairman) of the JCS acts not only as part of the collegial body but as a representative of his service and as a check or watchdog on the others. If this sounds like a very uneconomical operation—economic insanity to an economist—it is the way the real world is. It also illustrates the way in which we use the concept "economy"; as a system for producing and exchanging goods rather than as efficiency and minimization of cost. The inefficiency of the organization is not really all that uncommon.

[aa]Note the needs of a chief executive represent only one determinant of a central budget office's product, albeit the most important. The other determinants would be institutional role of the budget office (inasmuch as it differs from the chief executive's), and the demands and requests of the other agencies of government in the form of budget submissions. (In normative theory central budget offices do not have an institutional role distinct from the needs of the chief executive; but in the real world of *interface* organizational politics they try to strike a semi-detached professional pose.)

perceived changes in demand. Seldom did anyone perceive what was happening as purposive change of goals or niche.

Accordingly, budgeting evolved from accounting control, to improvement of administration and management, to policy planning and execution. Simultaneously, the nature of tasks and techniques as well as the types of personnel recruited have undergone sharp changes (accountants to general administrators to economists). With some distinct exceptions, these changes have been responses to depoliticized alterations in their environments.[bb] Of course, some newly developed techniques of budgeting have ended up having political consequences, but that is another matter too involved to take up here.[29]

If public organizations are viewed as procurers and processors of raw materials, and offerers of products at their boundaries, then their external economic exchanges (and internal economic structures) become more readily apparent. *The key distinction between economic and political factors lies in the matter of legitimacy and goal concerns.*

Supply and Demand Considerations. Specialized scarcities in the labor market may affect public organizations in a straightforward economic manner. A scarcity of personnel trained in computer technology would make it temporarily unfeasible for a public organization to compete for personnel in the labor market. This would lead it to delay changes in task accomplishment (internal economic matters) involving installation of computers. If such a delay would not affect its functional niche and legitimacy within its domain nor alter those internal authority patterns that relate to over-all goals and direction, it might be seen as an external economic impingement.

The competitive capacity of public organizations in recruiting personnel can generally be treated as an economic matter: For instance, many classes of personnel would prefer to be employed in the private sector if public sector is not offering competitive salaries. Yet, for other personnel, the public sector has greater drawing power. Where public organizations pay more to political appointees than the appointees could obtain in the private sector one can speak

---

[bb]For a discussion of these changes in budgeting and budget offices see Allen Schick, "The Road to PPB: The Stages of Budget Reform," PUBLIC ADMINISTRATION REVIEW 26, no. 4 (December 1966). The discovery of the political aspects of the above changes in budgeting is interesting and serves some interesting functions. But more important for purposes of accurate description and analysis is how the organization participants view these changes and react to them. If they see them as normal, nonthreatening, or inevitable and act accordingly, they should, for purposes of organizational analysis, be conceptualized as economic rather than as political. Naturally the analyst faces the problem of whether the actors *really* perceive an impingement as they say they do. Administrators play a role that leads them to deny that they are involved in politics. We have no easy answer to this age-old problem except to say that if a participant *says* he perceives an event in a certain way and then *acts* accordingly, in most analyses, that is about all that matters.

of a patronage pay-off.[cc] Where they pay less and still obtain services of a class they can be seen as having a security payoff (job security) or a purposive payoff (the idealism of the Peace Corps). There may be other possible distinctions. The point is merely that when one focuses upon an organization and its policy subsystem, many aspects of personnel administration that we traditionally think of as politics are more usefully seen as economic.

General macro-economic and manpower conditions can also affect a public organization. Full employment and an inflationary economy make it difficult for public organizations, with their generally lower status and lag in pay scales, to draw in desired personnel.

Because public organizations are largely service rather than manufacturing organizations, their cost structure is often tied closely to labor rates (Labor costs are a higher proportion of total costs). Manufacturing industries can substitute machines for labor, thus unit costs (cost per individual good produced) can be kept down even as wage rates move upward. Although computerization has had an immense effect upon those government agencies that have standardized rules and process information on large numbers of cases, public agencies are less amenable to mechanization. Because they must compete with private industry for labor, agencies sooner or later must raise their wage rates. Thus many public agencies (similar to private service organizations such as universities) find their unit costs, their costs of delivering services, spiraling upward. At least in part, the problems of labor procurement and the low substitutability of machines for men underlie the crises of urban finances and of agencies such as urban school systems in the late 1960s and early 1970s.

Macro-economic conditions sharply affect the workloads of some public organizations. In a period of recession and high unemployment, the workloads of welfare agencies, unemployment insurance divisions, and police departments may go up while that of Selective Service may decline as more men volunteer for service. Whether in contraction or expansion the general economy will affect the workload of such public organizations as the Departments of Commerce, Treasury, Labor, Agriculture, Internal Revenue Service, state departments of corporations, banking, insurance, real estate, revenue collection, alcoholic beverage control, public utilities, etc.

Natural disasters like hurricanes, floods, and tornadoes which necessitate

---

[cc]Note that patronage is commonly thought of as political, but unless the patronage is consciously aimed at influencing legitimacy and resources of a public organization we would treat it as economic. Until the Post Office encountered massive difficulties in recent times its extensive patronage appointments were more meaningfully treated as economic involving an exchange between organization and environment that was merely traditional. Questions of legitimacy were never seriously raised. Patronage was, however, an economic resource *for political parties* in building party allegiance, thus permitting the party to establish some control over policy goals. See James Q. Wilson's "Economy of Patronage," JOURNAL OF POLITICAL ECONOMY 69 no. 4 (August 1961): 369-80.

activation of a state's National Guard units or overtime schedules for police would properly be conceived of as a product-demand impingement on such public organizations. The effect of an epidemic upon a public health organization would fall into this same category. There is little chance that the legitimacy of a Guard's activation or the resulting expense would be questioned. But we need not turn solely to natural disasters. The popular increase in camping in America has brought great increases in the workload and changes in the internal economy (task structure and allocation of resources) of the National Park Service. Extensive expansion projects have been carried out. The naturalist skills of rangers are being supplemented by the skills of the policeman and the human relations expert. The increased demand for outdoor recreation that is bringing these changes is diffuse in origins and represents little identifiable, purposive behavior toward the National Park Service itself. This sort of demand is most usefully treated as economic, and considered political only if the translation of the demands into budgetary resources or statutes raises questions of legitimacy with regard to an agency's goals or directions.

Technological Innovation. Technological changes generally qualify as external economic factors. The Internal Revenue Service has undergone sweeping changes as a result of the development of computer technology; the Federal Aviation Agency as a result of the air traffic explosion and the development of extremely sophisticated radio-navigational equipment; segments of the army and the marines because of the helicopter; the navy's submarine service because of the missile-carrying Polaris submarine; and parts of the air force because of the Minuteman missiles. These technological changes are often far-reaching in their impact on an organization and may ultimately affect internal economy *and polity*. A key question for analysis concerns the conditions under which technological innovations are introduced. Some innovations do threaten conceptions of agency mission and become political matters. The most well-known example is that of the introduction of airplanes to the central missions of the military.

Manipulating Economic Input. Now let us turn to the other side of the external economic exchange picture—activities of public organizations designed to affect their economic environment. The most obvious examples are those in which a public organization seeks to find the most favorable economic conditions by competitive bidding and mass central purchasing. But public organizations such as the army, air force, or the Urban Mass Transportation Administration also try to overcome the hesitancy of suppliers and contractors of needed goods and services by offering "cost-plus-fixed-fee" contract arrangements, grants, loans, or by purchasing capital assets and leasing the same to them.[dd]

[dd]The obvious examples are in the aerospace industry which leased plants and machines tools from the air force. In the field of merchant marine shipping the United States

Stockpiling of raw materials or finished products in an effort to influence the general economy is more common in private industry but is done to some extent in the public sector (weapons and strategic material). There are instances in which public organizations create or stimulate suppliers of economic necessities: In establishing the Rand Corporation the air force gave birth to many research organizations that have supplied it and other public organizations with an economic good, informational analysis. And although there are political aspects to the FAA's sponsorship of a supersonic transport's development, the organization has tried from one perspective to create economic conditions that would supply its needed demand, i.e., situations in the field of aviation needing regulation and control. Thus, if we view any public organization as drawing upon its environment for inputs and converting them into products offered to clientele, we can readily see efforts to manipulate the external economic environment. The JCS may covertly strive at certain points to have Congress request their testimony, thus stimulating the demand for their own product. Or they may try to have a policy question suppressed or settled at a lower level, thus seeking to block product demand.

Conclusion

External political and economic patterns are the major determinants of organizational viability. Public agencies are nested in a set of political and economic structures and relations that determine and shape their long-run directions of change and their short-run interactions and concerns. Sooner or later, in any political system (sooner in a democratic one) changes in the sentiment distributions of the general public and the public in-contact flow through in-contact influentials to effect basic agency goals and legitimacy. At the same time the ability of agencies to accomplish their tasks is affected by the costs of the factors of production and the pattern of industry structure and competition originating in the larger societal economy.

Public administration must analyze the breadth and intensity of political support and opposition if it is to explain the directions of agency and policy change. It must also analyze an organization's environment for its dependencies and interdependencies with other organizations. Without retreating into an infinite regression, one must examine the pattern of support and opposition of an organization's "relevant others." What is *their* political economy? That way, the cumulative pressures for change and stability can be isolated. This can be important in analyzing a particular organization, but it becomes even more important in analyzing change and/or stability in a policy subsystem.

Maritime Administration's central task is to affect economic conditions surrounding ship building and the use of American flag vessels. The government has in the past built and leased ships to private agents to induce them to carry government supplies to war zones.

Agencies' adaptation to their political environments depend upon the pre-cariousness of their goals (centrality and ambiguity), the ease with which surveillance is carried out, the way in which funds and personnel are obtained, and the feedback loops that relate the organization to their environments. At the same time analysis of environments has to look at the demand for services, the processes in the society by which claims are presented, the changes in demand, and the methods of evaluating the effectiveness of organizational output.

Analyses also must examine the flow of resources, the problems and costs of obtaining the factors of production, the impact of increases in population or of economic cycles, and the distribution system necessary to deliver products to consumers. In capitalist countries the public agency competes with private organizations for these factors. Its costs and performance are related to its ability to compete externally. However, even in the most fully controlled totalitarian country, public organizations must offer incentives to motivate work, and tradeoffs must be made to determine which product lines and governmental services will be promoted and which starved. Although one may choose not to highlight the economic environment of agencies, to totally ignore it, as has been customary in public administration, is to miss a vital aspect of analysis.

3

The Internal Political Economy

It might be assumed that existing public administration theory (both classical and neoclassical) would be helpful in considerations of the internal political economy of public organizations. After all, PAT has been largely concerned with internal structures and processes. Nonetheless, its usefulness is surprisingly limited.[a]

Classical PAT's maxims are beliefs about structure and process which are supposed to maximize certain values for a specified (usually narrow) range of organizations. Neoclassical PAT attempts to bring empirical rigor to bear on the same questions to which classical PAT addressed itself. Both versions of PAT have their limited but real practical utility. Our framework, on the other hand, seeks to illuminate the key dimensions of function, structure, and processes (which are the context in which PAT's maxims can be applied).

PAT tells us something about ways of maximizing certain values for those public organizations that are relatively bureaucratic in structure. Because it has tended to focus on bureaucratic organizations, traditional PAT has not illuminated the widespread variances that exist in internal polities. It has assumed a pyramid that may vary somewhat in its steepness, or it has assumed something vaguely referred to as a controlling group.[1] The subject has been left pretty much at that level. PAT has largely focused upon increasing the efficiency of task accomplishment (internal economy) where goals are clear and basic means of task accomplishment are well articulated to those goals. It has ignored internal conflict, and the development of competing but contained factions, and the mechanisms, such as succession processes and choices, by which new directions are set or imposed. In general, it has ignored the continuing interaction of political and economic (task) structure and process. Clearly there exists a richer diversity in internal polities and economies than has yet been explicated.

Polity Structure and Process

The internal political structure of an organization is the structure of of authority and power and the dominant values, goals, and ethos institutionalized in that structure. The range of internal political structures is wide. Some organizations

aThe political economy framework is not put forward as being "better" than the traditional approach of PAT, rather as their functions being different. Classical PAT is primarily assertive or prescriptive; and neoclassical is conceptually closed off from environment and have democratic polities—ones in which the members of the organization, the subordinates, exert strong influence over the leaders, their presumptive super-ordinates, by accepting or rejecting them. Trade unions, political parties, social movement organizations, and voluntary clubs and associations usually have formal or informal methods of registering membership wishes. But in public agencies and private corporations, members (employees) are paid wages and the acceptance of the wage contract tends to subject the members to a hierarchial authority structure.[2]

Even though the wage relation narrows the possible range of internal polities for public agencies and private corporations, considerable variation still exists. Factions and coalitions based upon enduring cleavages may continue for generations; overall the organization may resemble a loose federation, rather than a unitary hierarchy; subordinate members and units may have access to resources that inside or outside of the agency give them power in relation to their nominal superiors.

The internal political structures of public agencies differ in one major regard from private organizations: Their executive cadres tend to be presented with a more limited range of goal and domain options. A major function of any executive cadre (ruling elite, dominant faction, control group) is the definition and interpretation of goals, mission, and niche. In public agencies, however, the range of alternatives is usually limited by mandating statutes and legislative and executive overview.

Nonetheless, for two reasons the executive cadre of public agencies do not become mere implementors of received mandates. First, these mandates may be vague, ambiguous, and extraordinarily complicated. Therefore, the values and perspectives of the cadre become touchstones for interpreting, highlighting, and realizing the mandate or policy. There remains room for the kinds of interpretations that mark the political function. Second, as the executive cadre identifies with the agency, its ethos and goals, it becomes concerned about its long-range survival, growth, and esteem. Because many public organizations are involved in pursuing commonweal values (that is, highly esteemed collective values of the society) their executive cadres are likely to identify their agencies as embodying high values. The survival and growth of their program becomes not only a precondition for sustaining executive careers (as in private corporations) but a means for pursuing higher (even sacred) values.

Basic Polity Functions

Responsibility for maintaining and developing agency goals and directions leads to four major political functions of the executive cadre: (1) They must develop

---

focused on control and task accomplishment, and thus limits its capability to deal with questions of politics and change. The function of classical and neoclassical PAT is one of telling managers how to control and produce or convey to others decision premises necessary for the same.

and define agency mission, ethos, and priorities.[3] (2) They must develop boundary-spanning units and positions to sense and adapt to environmental pressures and changes that affect the survival, growth, and legitimacy of the agency.[4] (3) They must insure the recruitment and socialization of an agency elite to maintain the coherence and pursuit of agency goals.[5] (4) They must set and maintain the major parameters of economy, harmonizing it with shifting goal priorities.

1. *Defining and interpreting goals and missions.* Internally the executive cadre must develop and maintain a consensus among elite factions. All the classic tactics of political leadership are to be found: developing and sustaining institutional myths and symbols; manipulation of symbols to obtain unity and quiescence; developing and nourishing a sense of mission; suppression, deprivation, or purging of individuals or groups who refuse to "play the game," and rewarding those who do.

2. *Creating and sustaining boundary-spanning roles.* For many public organizations, boundary-spanning roles are crucial because their environments are turbulent and the flow of resources must be negotiated. Unlike internal economic roles that seek to coordinate variables more or less under the agency's control, the internal polity roles of boundary-spanning seek to adjust to constraints and contingencies not fully controlled and depoliticized by the organization,[6] The internal polity must establish and maintain functioning boundary-spanning structures in order to effectuate the political exchanges we described in discussing external polity.

The tasks of boundary-spanning structures are (1) surveillance for the collection of vital data about the environment and its contingencies that might affect domain or survival; (2) monitoring the availability of financial and personnel resources for operation; (3) seeking to assure, if they are problematic, a steady supply of raw material and resources by coming to grips with surrounding organizational domains and niches;[b] (4) and working to assure adequate legitimacy for the ends and means of the organization by cultivation of allies, product receptivity, and "good feedback." Examples of boundary-spanning roles and structures in public organizations are the political executives, departmental secretaries, assistant secretaries, and some bureau chiefs;[c] planning units; fiscal officers, legislative liaison offices; press or public information offices; field representatives; and organizational representatives on interdepartmental committees. Other countries may play down boundary-spanning roles such as information offices, yet they institutionalize positions that have similar effects. For instance, in communist countries, various representatives of the ruling party may have surveillance positions built into the agency.

---

[b]To the extent these are secure the task becomes one of internal economy.
[c]Of course, many high-level civil service positions perform the same function. It is not the sole province of political appointees.

It should be pointed out that the internal economy cannot be protected without effective boundary-spanning structures performing their tasks properly. But economic boundary-spanning units are those which deal with the procurement of the factors of production—personnel, facilities, and equipment—given a definition of goals, domain, niche, and relationships to "others." Because we are seeking to clarify the *functions* of internal polity we think a useful distinction can be made between the function of *establishing* and *defining* boundary-spanning structures as they relate to political problems and the *ongoing* function of maintaining and protecting the economic core (see below).

3. *The recruitment and socialization of elites.* The executive cadre must face the question, "What sort of men do we need?" They must also establish processes for socialization that will shape and mold incoming elite members. This function is at a different level from simply seeking to assure a flow of the skills and techniques necessary for task accomplishment. The recruitment and socialization processes for elite cadre affect the general direction and indeed the survival of the organization—an institutional rather than instrumental set of processes. Selective Service draws its elite cadre from national guardsmen and military reservists, and has a clear pattern of socialization, preserving the paramilitary élan that has served it so well in past years in matters of niche maintenance and survival.[7]

The Forest Service draws upon forestry schools of land-grant colleges and carefully socializes its cadre.[8] Other examples of the high priority accorded this function might be: the Foreign Service (especially of earlier years) drawing on Ivy League, liberal arts, or political-science types; the Justice Department recruiting idealistic Ivy League law school products; the Department of Agriculture drawing personnel from land-grant colleges; and the military officer corps with its intensive socialization in academies. An assumption that public organizations merely tap into civil service pools for members of their cadre is totally unwarranted. Cadre recruitment and socialization appear to have definite patterns that vary from one organization to another. It is not too hazardous a hypothesis that organizations will find some means of being more selective about recruiting and training their cadre than is required by civil service. If they are legally required to be open about recruitment they will institute intensive socialization programs.[9] Moreover, the more an agency defends precarious values or has problems in maintaining elite cohesion, the more it will require intensive socialization programs for its potential cadre.

4. *Overviewing, controlling, setting the major parameters of the economy.* At some point rulers must check to see that their rules are being carried out: they must see if procedures and resources designed to achieve a given end are actually being employed and are achieving their ends; and they must see to it that it conforms to shifts in goals or adaptations of niche. To

some degree whether this function is treated as a political function or an economic one is a matter of taste. It is a key intersection between the internal polity and the internal economy.

In a rigidly hierarchical organization, administrators and supervisors are more purely economic in their functions the closer they are to the line or "processing" positions of the organization. For example, a supervisor of clerks in an Old Age and Survivor's Disability Insurance (OASDI) office overviews a basic task function of the agency, the processing of claims. He supervises the work flow, quantitatively and qualitatively. But as information from various offices is aggregated, higher authorities can begin to tell whether there is a changing pattern of claims, or whether resources are adequate. At each higher level the over-all functioning of the agency is more open to view. (Of course, if one is examining the political economy of the OASDI office, not the total agency, the supervisor's political functions would be analyzed.)

The four polity functions discussed are initiated and carried out by executive cadres to insure growth, survival, and adaptation. But it should be apparent that sometimes they fail. For example: goal consensus among the elite is seldom perfectly achieved (nor would it necessarily be "good" for the public if it were), "adequate" boundary-spanning units are not provided for; the elite are not always properly socialized. To some extent the manner in which an executive cadre performs these functions is dependent upon the *shape* of the internal political structure.

Variable Dimensions of Internal Polity

The shape of the polity, or internal political structure, is an outcome of several interrelated phenomena: the formal mandated structure; the problems of task accomplishment; results of the resolutions of past crises; and evolving leadership styles. Discussion of six key dimensions will help us profile variations in polities: (1) constitutions, (2) degree of goal consensus, (3) unity of authority, (4) patterns of subunit power, (5) patterns of demand aggregation—articulation and conflict resolution, and (6) patterns of leadership succession.

Constitutional Order. A constitution of a nation-state, primitive society, or complex organization is a reflection of basic norms about the ends and means of power—conceptions of legitimate purpose or goals, and conceptions of legitimate authority wielded in pursuit of them.[d] This dimension of organizations (and for

---

[d]This is very nearly a definition of political culture. See Samuel Beer and Adam Ulam, PATTERNS OF GOVERNMENT, 2d ed. (New York: Random House, 1962), p. 36.

that matter of nation-states) has received little attention.[e] No doubt the neglect stems from the fact that we simply do not have the analytical tools to handle such a protean subject.

Constitutions need not be written, but in the case of public organizations the written statutes, promulgated regulations, and various memoranda are a perfectly logical starting point for analysis. Documents that describe or represent the organization to outside actors, the public, or to new members are also primary sources. The formal and informal communications directed to a new member during his period of socialization and any histories of the organization, particularly those written by organizational members, are also revealing. Beyond these positive indicators, the identification of constitutional norms becomes more difficult. Because organizational constitutions set limits for behavior, organization participants may be unaware of them unless they are asked what would happen if the norms were violated. Or one can look for situations in which there has been a violation, conflict, withdrawal of resources from the violator, etc.

First, organizational constitutions determine what sorts of incentive exchanges exist or are possible for an organization—i.e., the amount of time, energy, and commitment it can expect from different members and what rewards they can expect in return.[10] This, of course, influences internal economy, but it can also directly affect over-all direction and goals. If the norms of exchange for an organization are fundamentally weak and nonbinding, its polity is probably quite fragile. Or if an organization is confronted with a need for drastic change that requires near-total commitment and yet its exchange system is solidly utilitarian or materialistic, its survival may be in doubt (unless the utilitarian returns for commitments are extraordinarily high, e.g., extra duty pay).

Second, constitutional norms indicate the range of discretion and decision responsibilities for organizational elite and mass. The keystone of Selective Service's constitution has historically been "local board autonomy." This set the general boundaries for action, established roles, and general ground rules for interaction in decision processes. Still a myriad of quiet but intense struggles ensued over the daily enactment of this constitutional norm. But the norm laid down the general rules of the game; the struggle was usually over the meaning of "local board autonomy" in practice and in specific instances. The 1965-70 difficulties of Selective Service illustrated the crisis for an internal polity when rhetorical and ideological adherence to a constitutional norm places it out of touch with its environment. Surface and rhetorical adherence to the norm of

---

[e]Most of the study of constitutional law in recent times is not really a study of the constitution as the fundamental normative order—an expression of political culture. Rather it is the study of the manifestation of it in court cases. The earlier and more traditional scholars had a broad view of the constitution as a reflection of a normative order. See Edwin S. Corwin, THE HIGHER LAW BACKGROUND OF AMERICAN CONSTITUTIONAL LAW (Ithaca, N.Y.: Great Seal Books, 1929). But with the behavioral revolution in political science, modern students have tended to drop this outlook.

"local board autonomy" in the face of glaring inequities and inconsistencies between boards nearly brought the organization to extinction.

The crisis also illustrates the problems that can be raised by the incentive system as imbedded in the constitution. One reason Selective Service tried to hold to "local board autonomy" was that its constitution called for nonpaid volunteers at the heart of the system. These volunteers needed the status and psychic incentive provided by "local board autonomy." Had the system possessed a material exchange system, it might have been able to apply enough policy guidance to eliminate the inequities and inconsistencies of local boards and thus cope with the crisis.

To merely mention examples of the ties between internal polity and basic constitutional norms: Could attorneys in the Civil Rights Division of the Department of Justice be effectively ordered to slow down desegregation in the late 1960s? Could National Guard officers be effectively ordered to take their units into riots without loaded weapons? In each organization there are informal but powerful constitutional norms militating against the over-all directions in which the organizations and their executive cadre may be attempting to move. Thus, these constitutional norms are at the heart of internal polity—the struggle over general direction and goals.

Third, constitutional norms set the organization's relationship to relevant others in its policy subsystem and the society at large. To whom is it responsible or most responsive and under what conditions? Does the Corps of Engineers have a responsibility to follow presidential policy guidelines on preservation of ecological balance or should it follow congressional demands for pork-barrel projects irrespective of ecological considerations? In peacetime the corps has no problem in choosing the latter because such a choice coincides with its *organizational* constitution even if at times it strains current interpretations of the United States Constitution. In wartime the corps constitution might call for reevaluating the question of to whom it is responsible, or what its priorities are.

Finally, constitutional norms specify the political foci of collective actions, i.e., the concerns falling within or without the zone of indifference of the organization and its subgroups. The foci of collective political action naturally include goals but also more broadly its domain, clientele groups, and, in general terms, the technology (which from a more immediate focus is an internal economic matter). It is the strength of such constitutional norms that often makes it disastrous for a new agency to be placed in an established department or an older one to be shifted to a different department. Often the established constitutional order of an adopting organization will not permit a widening of collective foci in a way that will assure the foundling agency the energy and resources it feels it must have to survive.[f]

---

[f]Obviously a different situation may occur when an organization absorbs another as a result of "imperialism."

Goal Consensus. One of the most revealing of analytic concerns about internal polity is the degree of consensus on goals that exists within an organization. Few organizations have complete internal unity on purpose or functional niche. Moreover, as previously noted, public organizations are particulary susceptible to penetration by external political influences which seek to alter their goals and/or niche. Every public organization will have its dominant faction (perhaps sustained by external actors) with its prevailing *Weltanschauung*.[g] The dominant faction may be challenged, however, and the intensity and manifestation of these conflicts are important subjects for analysis.

Conflicting views of goals and contending groups of elites may arise from a variety of sources: (1) from competing subunits seeking to move the organization in a direction that results in their aggrandizement, (2) from the ambiguity of the organization's statuory mandate that encourages differing interpretations, (3) from the machinations or intervention of external actors who seek to change its direction or niche, (4) from heterogeneity or disparateness within the elite cadre stemming from diverse recruitment channels and socialization processes, (5) from elite factions with external ties to a profession or functional speciality, (6) from the placement of a political executive with "new ideas" over high-ranking civil servants of long tenure, and (7) from operations that cover wide areas, and tasks that are complex, vague, or diverse.[11] Thinking of organizational goals in terms of monolithic unity is thus unwarranted.

Nor, as we note in point (7) above, can one assume monolithic consensus about the *means* of accomplishing tasks. Conflict over means is a natural outgrowth of perspective and values shaped by different roles. The old saw about the inseparability of means and ends is appropriate here. Conflicts over means often become so far-reaching in effects that they cross the boundary between internal economy and polity and alter the over-all direction of an organization.

An obvious example of internal conflict over direction and goals was the struggle within the United States Army over air power during the 1920s. The fight reached epic proportions, including the court martial of General "Billy" Mitchell. Ultimately the conflict resulted in establishment of a separate air corps and autonomy vis-à-vis the army. Other examples would be the struggle within a prison between elite factions favoring custodial goals and techniques and those favoring rehabilitation,[12] or mental hospitals and reform schools, where factions vie over custodial or treatment goals.[13]

---

[g]Studying business organizations Cyert and March spoke of dominant coalitions—coalitions of different divisions and subunits. It may be more appropriate at times to speak of dominant factions in public organizations, which are often heterogeneous statutory conglomerates. The loss of an entire unit might not affect the others within a department. This can even be said of many bureaus and divisions that are multifunctional. The choice of faction or coalition may depend on the level of analytical focus—department bureau or division. See R. Cyert and James March, A BEHAVIORAL THEORY OF THE FIRM (Englewood Cliffs, N.J.: Prentice-Hall, 1963), passim.

Unity of Authority. At first glance unity of authority may seem quite similar to goal consensus, but they are separable dimensions. An agency could have a splintered authority structure but consensus on goal among all factions, or it could have unity of authority but lack consensus on goal. Not all public organizations have a singular head and a unitary chain of command. Many are headed by commissions and boards. Those that function as true directing boards (rather than as figureheads) and fail to act in a united fashion tend to create coalition patterns that foster pursuit of multiple goals.

The California Board of Cosmetology in the 1960s was racked by a vicious fight between owners of beauty salons and hairdressing schools that were discounting prices. The split was manifest among board members and extended down into the organization. A state public utilities commission may be pulled in differing directions, with one commissioner vigorously pursuing regulation of the natural gas industry, another seeking to protect the industry from what he feels is overzealous regulation, and yet another pushing for tighter regulation of telephone companies. Certain subdivisions of such a public organization may become virtual fiefdoms of one commissioner or another. At the federal level, the Interstate Commerce Commission has been affected by internal divisions between those favorably disposed toward railroads and those favoring motor carriers and water carriers (supported respectively within ICC by the Bureau of Motor Carriers and the Bureau of Water Carriers and Freight Forwarders).[14]

Other public organizations represent conglomerations of functions that make cohesive authority a virtual impossiblity. Thrown together by statute or executive order they can only take on something like a federated pattern of authority. The relationships are tenuous at best between such disparate units within the United States Department of Agriculture as the Food and Nutrition Service, which administered the food stamp program, and the Cooperative State Research Service, which funds experimental stations.

The Commerce Department has been described as:

... congeries of independent bureaus ... all old establishments created prior to the Department itself. ... Each was an inbred Bureaucracy of its own. There was little department spirit or esprit de corps. Some of the bureaus even placed their own names on their letterheads, without mentioning the Department.[15]

Federated authority is more than a mere level of analysis problem stemming from studying conglomerate departments. If one descends to bureau and division levels, he will still find examples of patterns where one bureau chief or director is found at the top of an organization chart, but analysis reveals strong subunits and factions that act like units of a federal system, each with considerable inviolable autonomy.

Patterns of Subunit power. The foregoing discussion of authority only indicates what students and practitioners know—that the formal equality of subunits represented by a straight line on an organization chart is mythical. Subunits are responsible for different goals or for different phases of task accomplishment and, accordingly, they develop different interests and power capabilities. As noted earlier, some subunits draw upon support from outside the organization, but there are other bases of power. One of the primary bases of power lies in essentiality of function. Those subunits that are able to support a claim of essentiality, of critical and implacable need, are able to demand more attention and resources.

The FBI is well known for its overweening power within the Department of Justice. This power has not been based solely on the charismatic leadership of its former director, J. Edgar Hoover, and skillful public relations, but has rested in large part upon its essentiality and primacy of its function. Law breakers cannot be apprehended and cases cannot be prosecuted without investigation and enforcement. Prosecutions by divisions of the Department of Justice depend upon information provided by the bureau. Its work is essential to the functioning of the entire department.[h]

Essentiality may partly rest upon a subunit's unique epitomization of the entire organization's mission. The fighter bomber squadrons of a Tactical Air Command wing are no more essential than the maintenance squadron to successful completion of the wing's mission. But because they epitomize the entire wing's mission—the delivery of weapons to target—the operational squadrons are likely to have first claim on resources and more influence over policy.

Another source of subunit power variations is access to, and influence over, information and communications both with the environment and internally. McCleery, speaking of the importance of communication patterns, goes so far as to say, "communication patterns serve as one functional equivalent for force in sustaining the power structure of a stable society."[i] Those who control communications and have access to information are able to react before others to define situations and to make a communications input that will sustain definition. Thus it is that an adjutant's or administrative services office in military organizations has power out of all proportion to any formal description or idealized conception of its place in the hierarchy. The adjutant's office is a central receptor and dispensor of organizational communications and speaks authoritatively "for the commander." Similarly, fiscal offices of government departments hold unusual power for mere "staff offices." Comptroller's offices,

---

[h]The department has roughly thirty-three thousand employees, fifteen thousand of whom work for the FBI.

[i]Richard H. McCleery, "Policy Change in Prison Management," in COMPLEX ORGANIZA-TIONS: A SOCIOLOGICAL READER, ed. Amitai Etzioni (New York: Holt, Rinehart & Winston, 1964), p. 377. The standing joke in many organizations that the secretaries have "the real power" is only partly apocryphal. Any power they do have is based largely upon their access to information and communications. See David Mechanic, "Organizational Power of Lower Participants," ADMINISTRATIVE SCIENCE QUARTERLY 7, no. 3 (December 1962): 349-64.

research and development units, budget offices, and long-range planning units gain much of their power from controlling information and definitions relevant to functioning. Simon, Smithburg, and Thompson offer an example of the importance of communications control to subunit power in their discussion of the struggle over "who is to be permitted to communicate with whom" in the Office of Price Administration.[16]

Demand Aggregation and Conflict Resolution. Internal polities of public organizations vary in the patterned expression of *demands* by subunits, lower-level membership, or elite factions. In organizations as in nation states the patterns of demands for change are shaped by the social and economic resources of strata and groupings. Demand patterns do not deal solely with political matters. The polity may handle many demands that are instrumental or matters of internal economy, e.g., demands for longer breaks from the tedious work in a government arsenal. Indeed, most wage-and-benefit demands are economic matters. They involve minor adjustments in the organization's incentive system. But the *patterns* of demand articulation-aggregation are the objects of our concern, not the demands themselves, and the *patterns* are in aspect of internal polity. They reflect the underlying distribution of power. They shape the direction, goals, and functional niche of a public organization. They determine responsiveness of the organization to change, its vulnerability to hostiles and competitors or to internal pressures and, indeed, its capacity to survive.

The pattern of demand aggregation and internal conflict is shaped by several factors such as subgroup and organizational identity and cohesion, perceived grievances, and the relative costs and benefits of expressing grievances.

Subgroup identify and cohesion are reflected in the kinds of employee associations that develop. Some public organizations are unionized, their members are loyal to their union, and they have highly developed channels from shop stewards to the top of the union hierarchy. Contract negotiations are binding and strike threats are used as weapons directed against the organization's elite. Other agencies (usually with a lesser proportion of blue-collar employees) have employee associations, which aggregate demands and articulate them not only to the organization elite but also to legislative committees that control appropriations or salaries.[j] The associations become primarily lobbying agencies.

In some public organizations the lower-level membership is so dispersed geographically, fractionated in terms of interests, or lacking in bonds of unity that there is scarcely a discernible pattern of demand aggregation-articulation. Others readily develop group channels. The close interaction patterns, high-pressure and critical nature of air-traffic controllers' work provides for a unity that makes it rather easy for them to develop a pattern of aggregation-

---

[j]Not all government salary matters have been placed under civil service. The most notable exception at the federal level has been the Post Office, which, until recently, set postal salaries "in conjunction with" the House Post Office and Civil Services Committee.

articulation, but general GS-9's thru GS-12's (middle-level administrators in the same organization) may find it more difficult. Some public employees have a self-perception that is highly professional, elitist, and individualistic. Therefore, they are slow to act in any concerted effort to register demands, but when they do so they may act with unusually high beliefs in the appropriateness of their action. Foreign Service Officers probably fit this category and their signing of an anti-Cambodian "incursion" resolution in the Spring of 1970 was a manifestation of their deeply felt frustrations with the conduct of the Vietnam war.

The kinds of grievances that are expressed by different groups and individuals will reflect the bases of members' identification with the organization. Where members are just "holding down a job," grievances will largely concern "bread-and-butter" concerns: salary, work conditions, job security, pension arrangements. On the other hand, where there is high identification with the commonweal values embodied in the organization, the grievances may concern themselves with the distance between goals and actual procedures and accomplishment. The grievances of air-traffic controllers and the foreign service officer in the examples above were of this type.

It is also necessary to examine the costs and benefits of expressing demands. Where employees are not insulated from superordinate control, expression of grievances can lead to dismissal, demotions, or the stunting of careers. The maverick military officer who has an effectiveness report written on him twice a year by his immediate superior is less likely to be recommended for promotion. In general, only as professional and employee associations become legitimate and established does the expression of grievance become accepted and regular. Where these forms are not present, grievance-demands are expressed subrosa in griping patterns, informal withdrawals of support or "sabotage," and in the formation of cliques and sub-rosa counter-elite factions.

The nature and structure of the organization's work, i.e., its internal economy, may have a great deal to do with the channels chosen by the leadership of union or employee groups in demand aggregation-articulation. The work of some organizations involves professional groups of high specialization and the resulting channel of demand aggregation may be through the national professional body and back to the dominant elite of a public organization. On the other hand, the sprawling geographic dispersion of postal workers and generally nonprofessional nature of the work led to development of a centralized "in-house" union. In some organizations demands that will affect over-all direction and goals may be aggregated through overhead staff officers such as budget or personnel, while in other organizations they may flow through line executives to the top.

As grievances and demands flow through an agency they are channeled into more or less institutionalized decision centers and conflict-resolving mechanisms. Some conflicts may have to be resolved outside of the agency by bargaining among relevant others; in the meantime the agency is paralyzed. The ability or inability of an organization to resolve conflict, or the level at which it can resolve it, vitally affects its direction and existence. Some organizations develop a pattern of appealing conflicts among subunits to a higher authority, so that everything "ends up in the secretary's or director's office." Some develop a pattern in which subunits negotiate settlements without going to higher levels. They may agree not to disagree, and institutionalized decision rules may resolve conflicts. These decision rules take the form of asking for everything that everyone wants; redefining a problem so that it is no longer such; or developing a log-rolling pattern in which they support one another's demands in turn. Other agencies may have special intra-agency committees and quasi-judicial councils for resolving internal conflicts.

It is worth noting that the literature of PAT barely touches on these issues. What is sorely lacking is a typology of issue and conflict-resolving mechanisms within agencies that would parallel our knowledge of the demand aggregation and conflict-resolving mechanisms in the society and in legislative arenas.[17]

Leadership Succession, Cadre Recruitment, and Socialization. The structure of the executive cadre—including those who appoint it, those who establish criteria for dismissal, promotion, and transfer—often is set in the external polity of a public agency. The structure of the cadre (terms and time of office) and the homogeneity of the membership then become key determinants of the unity, coherence and cohesion of an agency effecting policy and performance.

That the top leadership of a public organization is formally selected by persons or institutions external to it makes the succession pattern no less important to and *perhaps* no less a reflection of internal polity. What may seem to be merely the external imposition of a procurator is often an established pattern which reflects a synthesis of internal as well as external forces.

Students of the federal governmental structure tend to emphasize that cabinet appointments seek to satisfy the interest groups that surround a department. This is probably only one side of the coin; the other is the need to satisfy the expectations of the public organization's elite. We tend to overlook their importance because these expectations are so similar to external interests. For example, consider the impact on the morale of the Department of Health, Education, and Welfare if Barry Goldwater, noted for his stand against federal welfare spending, had been appointed as its secretary in 1968. Robert Finch, one of the most liberal members of the Republican party, found the position to be painful, and his legitimacy difficult to sustain, with the liberal program-enthu-siasts within the department's elite. Except when external political powers are trying to drastically change an agency, the succession patterns of public organizations are likely to reflect internal expectations as well as external choices.

Appointments often are actually part of a circulatory system of elite careers. Though presidents technically appoint all political executives, studies have shown that the agency head is the central figure in the selection process and that he tends to draw upon agency cadre, especially as the regime settles in office.[18] A large portion of top leadership spots in the federal government are filled by promotions within the cadre. A Brookings Institution study of the top 180 positions in the federal government between 1933 and 1965 showed that only 15 percent of the appointees had no previous federal service; 35 percent had held career jobs, with 14 percent having served in the same agency in which they were appointed political executives; 61 percent had held previous political appointments at the federal level, 24 percent in the same agency. Some organizations have large proportions of "internal appointments." Forty-one percent of the State Department's leadership positions went to careerists within, 28 percent in agriculture, 22 percent in the FCC. Forty-nine percent of the Department of Justice's top positions went to departmental noncareerists, 41 percent of Agriculture's, and 36 percent of Treasury's.[19] The trend is toward appointment of more career officials, thus increasing promotions from within cadres.[20] At the state and local levels the dependence upon internal appointments is even greater. Even when an appointment seems to be made from outside the appearance may be deceptive; it may merely ratify the nominee of an internal succession pattern.

Patterns of appointing a chief executive from within the cadre may include a "crown prince" system in which the chief executive chooses and trains his successor; a "stand-off" or consensus successor agreed upon by conflicting factions which share an informal veto; a "new majority" successor which represents a newly formed dominant faction or coalition; or spasmodic and clandestine coups.

The particular pattern of succession or changes in it grow out of three factors. First, the power distribution among subunits affects the succession pattern. Centralized power tends to produce crown prince patterns and federated power tends toward consensus successors. The degree of centralization also affects the tactics and shape of the counter-elite, offering alternatives to the dominant faction or coalition. They may range from cliques that are identifiable but with no purpose, through tightly organized cabals with intensely held purposes, to "shadow cabinets" ready to take over.

Second, the degree of consensus about the adequacy of organizational performance and the focus of discontent shapes the succession pattern. A discontented sovereign may send a procurator or a "new expert"; an intensely discontented minority faction in the top bracket of the elite cadre may produce a coup; or more extensive discontent may produce a consensus successor or a "new majority."

Finally, succession patterns are shaped by elite perceptions of what constitutes "standard" versus "deviant" career channels. The greater the discontent with organizational performance or the greater the rate of organizational change, the more deviant career patterns tend to be acceptable.[21]

Admiral Hyman Rickover, acerbic, intellectual, rebellious, Jewish, and with little sea experience, rose to unprecedented heights for a man of his characteristics and career pattern. He did so largely because he was needed in the development of the nuclear submarine program. General Bernard Schreiver also rose through a deviant career (relatively little flying and combat) to head the Air Force's Systems Command largely on the basis of his engineering background. On the other hand, police chiefs until recently have followed a rigid and unchanging career pattern of rising slowly from the ranks and rotating through certain divisions.

In summary, traditional PAT has not begun to provide the concepts and schemata for analyzing the rich variations in the internal polities of organizations—the widely varying ways in which the authority surrounding the over-all goals and directions of an organization is organized. It may be that the six dimensions of variation discussed above should be used to develop a classificatory schema. Perhaps organizations should be classified on the basis of the level of politicization—how prominent is internal polity as opposed to internal economy? Or put another way, to what degree are resources and energies directed toward influencing the authority pattern that covers the over-all goals, directions, and life processes of an organization?

Internal polities might be classified as pluralistic, oligarchic, gerontocratic, revolutionary authoritarian, modernizing democratic. A scheme might combine some description of power distribution, the manner in which it is wielded, and something of the ethos of the dominant faction. Or we might have to treat each of the foregoing as a different dimension. Regardless, the need seems apparent. The power system as it relates to over-all goals, directions, and major organizational parameters is a central element of public organizations.

Production Task System

At the heart of every organization is a "suborganization whose 'problems' are focused upon effective performance of the technical function."[22] The main concern of persons filling the cluster of roles in the internal economy are the "exigencies imposed by the nature of the technical task . . . "; problems growing out of the nature of the raw materials to be processed; the division of work and responsibilities so that the cooperation required for task accomplishment is forthcoming; allocating resources and maintaining an incentive system to accomplish tasks, and doing so efficiently or bringing about changes that will. Public organizations, no less than private, must coordinate behavior and allocate resources in order to produce an output that satisfies relevant others.

It is the economic aspect of organizations (under different labels) that has been the major concern of traditional and neoclassical PAT. The economic aspect has thus received the most analysis, dissection, prescription, and attention. But for all this, the advance toward a systematic, empirical theory of public administration has been disappointing. A primary factor seems to have been a lack of sensitivity to the political-economic distinction and an inability to analyze and classify dimensions of task and technology.

It is the internal economy in which the technological aspects (in a broad sense) of the organization are concentrated, where instrumental and efficiency norms take precedence over legitimacy. In the realm of internal economy, role incumbents are likely to consider problems of over-all direction and survival as "someone else's business."

Assuming scarcity and some orientation to achieve goals, organizations seek to optimize efficiency within the internal economy.[k] To the extent that public organizations are subject to budget constraints and output evaluation, some drive to efficiency can be expected. The pursuit of efficiency may require alteration of major characteristics or behavior of an organization, a possibility that links this concern of internal economy very closely to internal and external political processes and structures.

Buffering the Technological Core

Since organizations exist to accomplish work, the organizational polity must protect and insulate the technological core from external contingencies, both political and economic, that would disrupt task accomplishment. The organization buffers out factors that disturb a constant and routine state of affairs by smoothing and standardizing input and output flows, or by forecasting impinging fluctuations and scheduling adjustments.[23]

Buffering can be done in a government arsenal or power and water project, as it would be done in private industry, by stockpiling raw materials on the input side and "warehousing" on the output side. A motor vehicle pool, a government-operated airline, or the United States Mint buffers by use of scheduled preventive maintenance. Careful recruitment by the personnel office of lower level workers with the right specialized skills and the production of homogeneity

---

[k]One of the standard complaints against public bureaucracies is that they do not, in fact, optimize efficiency, that there is little incentive for cost cutting and prudent allocation of resources. Studying a related problem, Louis Pondy has shown that industries where owners are heavily involved in management are less likely to hire extra staff than industries where owners are not as heavily represented. Presumably owners seeking profit have less of a "taste" for additional staff than managers whose incomes are not clearly related to profits. See Louis Pondy "Effects of Size, Complexity, and Ownership on Administrative Intensity," ADMINISTRATIVE SCIENCE QUARTERLY 14, no. 1 (1969): 47-61. In the absence of market constraints and profit incentives, the degree of drive to efficiency upon the part of executive cadres cannot be assumed. In the American case, the drive to efficiency is often imposed by a separate public agency (at either the state, national, or local level) that reviews the internal management, workloads, and work arrangements.

by on-job-training programs are a means of buffering.[1] In some political systems the development of civil service for mass-organization positions was an attempt to buffer internal economies from the vagaries of extraneous contingencies and from personnel with political connections but few task-related skills. In the American system, with patronage now largely confined to high-level, political-executive positions, most public organizations have been able to buffer their personnel requirements.

Another means of enhancing efficiency and protecting the internal economy or technical core is to expand organizational jurisdictions and functions to encompass crucial contingencies. In the private sector an example springs readily to mind—auto manufacturers develop dealerships to buffer their distribution problems, and on the input side they move into steel manufacture and fabrication. In the public sector there are manifestations of the same phenomena, though we are not accustomed to thinking of them as such. Take the example of the United States Justice Department's efforts to control the contingencies that impinged on its ability to assure the right to vote. The department had sought legislation that would permit it to bring suit against voter registrars who discriminated rather than to leave the burden of suing upon the aggrieved citizen. This statutory green-light was given to it in the Civil Rights Act of 1957.

Faced with a rash of delaying and evading tactics, the department sought authority to continue suing registrars who resigned to evade prosecution. They supported authorizing the federal courts to appoint referees where they found a pattern of discrimination. This was obtained in the Civil Rights Act of 1960.

But the department found its internal economy disrupted by another uncontrollable contingency—the federal district judges in "hard core" segregationist areas, who often refused to send in referees. The department was also frustrated by counties that, with the acquiescence of federal district judges, changed their election laws in a kaleidoscopic manner. As a result, the department sought and obtained, in the 1965 Voting Rights Act, authority for the attorney general to order federal registrars into "hard core" areas *without* going through the courts, and a ban on election law changes unless approved by the attorney general or a federal court of the District of Columbia. Thus, faced with disruptive contingencies to its internal economy, the department responded by extending its functions and jurisdictions (Thompson would say, "its domain") to encompass and control them.[m] The case provides a good example of how a matter of internal economy arises and spills over into the external political quadrant.

Public organizations seeking to change people often seek to enhance the

---

[1] Recruitment of mass-organization members is emphasized here. It is an economic matter. Recruitment of elite cadre is more likely a political matter.

[m] Of course, the department was not the only party seeking the change.

operation of the internal economy by encompassing the object worked upon, in order to monitor it more closely, control it and its environment, or generally cope with contingencies it may create. Narcotic rehabilitation centers, military academies, mental hospitals, veterans administration hospitals all induct their material for total participation in the organization.[24]

Another means of protecting the production task system is to expand clientele. We often think of public organizations as serving assigned clientele (Social Security, Veterans Administration) or of their expansion as a function of "empire building." But not all public organizations have preordained clientele, and forces other than empire building may be at work. An agency that applies standard techniques to large populations may have considerable organizational slack resulting from putting in new equipment. If a state's criminal identification and investigation files are computerized and automated, the machinery will be designed to handle existing load plus future growth. The resulting slack may be a temptation and/or embarrassment that motivates client expansion. The Veterans Administration runs television and radio public-interest bulletins urging veterans to apply for benefits, Social Security urges the elderly to inquire about benefits, and Ray Charles tells anyone who feels they have been discriminated against to contact the Equal Employment Opportunity Commission. The manifest rationale is to alert citizens to benefits that are rightly theirs.[n] But it is possible that other forces such as domain adjustments are at work.[25]

Sometimes excess technological capacity and the slack it creates is dealt with by diversification. Slack is particularly dangerous for a public organization because it makes it vulnerable to charges of waste and obsolescence. In the late 1950s and early 1960s, as draft calls fell to record lows, Selective Service obtained authority to service and maintain the records of standby reservists. It also pressed unsuccessfully for a role in civil defense mobilization. Efforts such as these, while taken to maintain the size and capability of the internal economy, can very quickly effect external polity.

Not all public organizations are able to protect their technological core from environmental buffeting. To the extent that they cannot, they lose economies of scale, advantages of specialization in personnel, programs, and equipment, incur high coordination costs, and run the risk of collecting bad accounting information. They may suffer generally from weak controls, empire building by members of the elite, and low efficiency.[26] They may be no less valued and valuable, merely less efficient.

Task Structure

Structure refers to the patterned interaction of subunits and roles. It has its origins in the task of the organization—the requirements of the job. The two

---

[n]It is an interesting aspect of American political culture that welfare benefits typically have not been advertised. Apparently we viewed some citizens and benefits as more rightly joined together than others.

major aspects usually treated are hierarchy and coordination. Often we have sought the "one best way" to coordinate and divide responsibility and authority. Had we been more sensitive to structure being largely an outgrowth of technological and task requirements, our efforts might have been more fruitful.

Dimensions of Technologies and Tasks. Organizations vary widely in their technologies. Focusing upon the implications of technologies for interdependence and coordination, James Thompson identifies three major varieties of technology: long-linked, mediating, and intensive.

(1) Long-linked technologies are those in which acts are *serially* interdependent with each activity geared to the requirement of the next, as in the case of the mass-production assembly lines (government arsenals, army basic training centers, navy shipyards). A long-linked technology may be made up of just a few serially connected tasks or may, depending upon the complexity of the product and the divisibility of task, be divided into subparts, which may, in turn, be divided in two major subtypes, batched and continuous processing, depending upon whether partially transformed raw materials can be stored without damage to their final production. Batch and continuous-processing technologies require different buffering forms. An army basic training center has a continuous processing, long-linked technology. Trainees cannot easily be stored or recycled without their morale being damaged. Though the army tries to avoid damaging morale by strict attention to the input and output sides of their organization, it still occurs and creates the infamous stereotype of a "hurry-up-and-wait" army.

Government arsenals typically have batched long-linked technologies. So does the Internal Revenue Service with its deluge of inputs on April fifteenth that can then be batched and handled piecemeal over the year; or the Central Intelligence Agency, which takes in a glut of raw material in the form of U-2 or spy satellite photographs, which are then batched and processed as they seem to be needed for different types of policy problems.

(2) Mediating technologies attempt to link clientele seeking interdependence or link clientele with goods and services, either operation requiring standardized procedures applied extensively to multiple clients distributed in time and space (welfare departments, Social Security Administration, the National Labor Relations Board, state employment offices).

(3) Intensive technologies entail the application of a variety of techniques to achieve a change in some object with the selection of technique being determined by *feedback* from the object itself (prisons, mental hospitals, veterans administration hospitals, military academies).[o] As we shall

---

[o]Students of organizations have been actively engaged in studying the effects of technologies upon organizations and attempting to develop typologies of them. Though it is incomplete, as Thompson noted in his book, his is one of the more illuminating typologies.

note later, this typology has profound implications for forms of coordination.

Organizational technology and the way it links tasks together are related to the characteristics of the nature of the raw material handled; their volatility and variability, and the clarity and precision of means-ends relationship. If raw materials (for some public agencies, clientele) cannot be standardized, each batch or case may require separate handling, and standardization is difficult.

The degree of routinization and standardization, in turn, affects the skill composition of agency personnel and the degree to which lower-level personnel perform economic rather than political tasks. For instance, many governmental agencies have mediating technologies in which the agencies (Federal Communication Commission, Interstate Commerce Commissions) essentially sift applicants for licensing or subsidies. If the criteria of allocation could be completely standardized, awards could be made by computer processing. In the absence of such standardization, hearing examiners must weigh evidence and presentation against a set of multiple criteria. If the franchise or subsidy is significant, the hearing officer may be playing a vital political role in interpreting goals and policies.[27]

Specialization and differentiation within an organization are functions not only of technology but also of the variety of "products" offered by the organization, the scope of operations needed to produce and distribute "production" to clientele, and the geographic dispersion of the organization. The Department of Commerce offers a wide variety of "products," commercial statistics, nautical charts, patents and trademarks, weather forecasts, standardization of weights and measures, aid to redevelopment areas, conciliation of civil rights disputes, stimulation of tourism, scientific data, highway improvement funds, a merchant marine, pilotage on the Great Lakes, determination of resource requirements for defense, supervision of the St. Lawrence Seaway, and coast and geodetic surveys. The deceptively simple chart of the department hides enormous complexity.

There is a wide variation among public organizations in the scope of operations necessary to deliver a product. By scope we mean the range of basic tasks, or subproducts, necessary to produce the major output. Scope alone can become a potent force in shaping internal economy. Compare the scope of the TVA and Selective Service. The former's "product for consumers" as defined by statute is development of the Tennessee River and its tributaries in the interest of navigation, flood control, electric power, and production of experimental chemical fertilizers; Selective Service's is to provide the manpower necessary for national security consistent with a functioning economy.

Both have wide geographic dispersion; in fact, Selective Service's is greater than TVA's. Yet, it is TVA that must carry out a wider scope of operations to deliver its product. It must survey sites, build dams, powerhouses, and erect transmission lines; purchase coal for steam plants; sell bonds; sue and be sued; deal in real estate and personal property; exercise eminent domain; purchase coal for steam plants; develop rainfall and river-level data and supervise reservoir release programs; plan and engineer navigational development of the river; carry out forestry, fish, and game programs; develop and maintain recreational areas; handle contracts for power sales to hundreds of municipalities, cooperatives, private utility companies, large industrial firms, and defense production facilities; operate the Muscle Shoals fertilizer plants and distribute the product to nearly all states; and maintain cooperative relations with hundreds of state and local governmental agencies, private groups, unions, etc. Its operations are of wide scope.

Selective Service operates in all fifty states, Guam, and Puerto Rico, yet its scope of operations is relatively narrow. It merely registers, classifies, inducts, or defers registrants, maintains files, and carries out such correspondence and/or board meetings as are necessary. The registrants must come to deal with one of the four thousand plus boards and/or clerks that are the heart of the system. State and national headquarters plan, coordinate, monitor, and control their actions. Our intention is not to oversimplify Selective Service's operations. Yet, the contrast between the scope of TVA and the Selective Service is impressive. The difference between the Selective Service and the TVA would be reflected in the lists of occupational titles and the numbers and kinds of departments in the two organizations. The array of specialized functions and skills that TVA must juggle is immense and the scope of operations required by its goals emerges as a prime factor.

Organizations may have similar scope but differ widely in geographic dispersion. The TVA and the Army Corps of Engineers have strikingly similar "products to deliver to consumers"; the one stark difference is geographic dispersion.[P] TVA must operate in only seven states, the corps in fifty, plus some foreign operations. Because of its dispersion, the corps is seldom able to think in the intensive "basin development" terms of TVA. So rather than following this more broadly comprehensive way of conceptualizing their product, they tend to respond to the more immediate demands of congressmen and local interests.

Geographic dispersion can create very real problems in communications, coordination, and cohesiveness for a public organization; problems that its internal economy must somehow solve.

Coordination and Hierarchy: Grouping Principles. Thompson identifies three major types of subunit or role interdependence and resulting patterns of coordination.[28] (1) Pooled interdependence refers to circumstances where each unit contributes to the whole but none is directly dependent on the other. Each

---

[P]The tasks of the two balance out in scope and diversity. The corps has a wider range of engineering tasks to perform but does not have to produce and distribute power and fertilizer.

contributes to task accomplishment, and thus the over-all effectiveness of the whole organization is dependent upon each part. But one unit can make its contribution without being directly dependent upon another unit. This inter-dependence can be handled at least cost by standardization—the establishment of rules and routines to be followed by all and requiring few communications and decisions. For example, in a geographically dispersed unemployment agency, clerks in each office can be taught the same rules and procedures and each office can make a contribution to the common task of processing claims. However, clerks within an office and offices within the agency are substantially inde-pendent of each other. (2) Sequential interdependence refers to circumstances of direct dependence. A must act before B can act, and unless B acts, A's effort is essentially wasted. Sequential interdependence is coordinated through planning and the establishment of schedules for action. If the flow-through of work is completely standardized, a plan or schedule operates like a standardized rule; however, variations from routine require adjustments of schedules and contin-gency planning. The costs in decisions and communications are higher than in pooled interdependence. (3) Reciprocal interdependence means the outputs of A become the inputs for B, and the outputs of B the inputs for A. Coordination is by mutual adjustment and energy-attention costs are high.

The different requirements of coordination have a direct relationship to how roles are grouped together in units and how units are related to each other in hierarchic patterns. Who reports to whom, what units are tied together under common authority, is partly a function of the drive to lower costs of coordination. The most intensive forms of reciprocally interdependent positions must be linked under one authority, for coordination costs would mount rapidly if problems of adjustment could not be resolved within a unit. Thus, even if A and B are at distant points geographically, or have different professional skills, their interdependence requires that they be grouped under a common authority. Coordination by schedule or plan is less constant and intensive than by mutual adjustment. Thus positions that are sequentially interdependent may not be grouped within one unit; they may coordinate across lines of authority, or be tied together at several steps removed. Whether sequential positions and units are in one unit or different ones depends upon aspects of technology, such as the ease of surveillance and the range of skills involved. Finally units having mainly pooled interdependence are grouped by geographic region or by skill to ease surveillance.

When an agency is responsible for several different products, the relationship among divisions still rests largely upon the costs and benefits of coordination. Some effort is usually made to locate programs and divisions close together at a low enough level to permit both conflict resolution at the lowest level possible and coordination of their program and planning interfaces. For instance, if a new kind of urban renewal or model cities program is developed, it will be hierarchically located so as to connect easier to other urban redevelopment prorams rather than to general housing or money-market units.

The analysis of the impact of these different dimensions upon internal economy must be explored as part of the development of our knowledge of other parts of the political economy paradigm; hopefully it will all take us further toward PAT than we have been able to move so far. Past research provides some clues as to the impact of the dimensions that seem to merit attention. Holding other factors constant, as differentiation increases the effective span of control decreases. Complexity stemming from wide scope (holding size constant) apparently requires more supervisory and administrative personnel.[29] Further, the more nonroutine the tasks, the more pressure there is to grant discretion to lower-level personnel, a trend that can upset equilibrium if not specifically countered by socialization and supervisory devices.[30] The political-economy paradigm accommodates and is bolstered by the considerable literature that has been developed on such control devices.[31]

Classical PAT sought to discuss how work should be organized (purpose, process, clientele, and area). Neoclassicists convincingly showed that no clear principle of organizing and grouping work had been uncovered by their predecessors. But the neoclassicists represented by Simon took a social psychological approach, so that they also failed to explain *how* organizations tend to be organized and why they follow the patterns they do.[q] J.D. Thompson seems to have suggested a major part of the answer and one which can better contribute to the building of an empirical theory of public administration. To the extent that norms of efficient task accomplishment prevail, an internal economy's patterns of coordination and hierarchy are shaped primarily by technologies and task dimensions.

In analyzing the impact of the internal economy on technology, coordination, and buffering patterns, Thompson's work persuasively focuses our attention on grouping priorities. Then one turns to considerations of diversity of products, scope of operations, and geographic dispersion. Which of these dimensions of internal economy is more important depends partly upon the object or unit of analysis chosen. The cabinet-level departments with their "holding company" heterogeneity makes diversity among products an obviously important consideration; but, for example, if one has as his object of analysis the National Security Agency, which makes and breaks codes, technology may be all-important in mapping out its internal economy. And it should be noted that the patterns of hierarchy and coordination adopted by an organization for its internal economy are not always a mere reflection of the "state of the art," but also of the amount of competition from rivals, political pressures

---

[q]Simon and others concentrated on managements' perspective but took a scientific approach. Some lines on page 37 of Simon's ADMINISTRATIVE BEHAVIOR capture the approach—"What is a scientifically relevant description of an organization? It is a description, that so far as possible, designates for each person in the organization what decisions that person makes and the influences to which he is subject in making these decisions." This approach might eventually provide an analysis and description of internal economy but through a torturously roundabout route, and results would be hard to "tie out" to a more global perspective.

from proximal others, and the outlook of organizational elites. Nonetheless, an analyst can profit by beginning his analysis of internal economy with the requirements of technology and basic tasks.

The structure of the internal economy represents an authoritative arrangement of positions and units so as to solve the problems of interdependence and organizational control. But it is an arrangement of power or authority that operates at the instrumental and efficiency levels rather than on the level of legitimacy and survival, that is, the level of the economic rather than of the political. Naturally, internal economy affects internal polity, and often the two power systems intersect, with interacting role incumbents merely worrying about different sets of problems or the same problem in different lights. The shape of the internal economy influences the many facets of organizational polity; the pattern of subgroup power; unity of authority; goal consensus; patterns of demand aggregation-articulation and conflict resolution; recruitment, socialization, and succession of elites.

Resource Allocation and Incentive Systems

Both public and private agencies use budgets and internal accounting procedures for internal allocating of resources. Wildavsky asserts that a budget is a behavioral contract imposing mutual obligations and controls upon the contracting parties.[32]

Viewed in this light, budgeting and accounting systems are vital mechanisms for maintaining the level of activity and types of cooperation necessary for efficient task accomplishment. (They may also be used in a polity struggle to reward and punish political factions and bring about changes. But here we mean to single out their economic importance.)

Accounting systems record variable data that communicate trends in resource-utilization efficiency, effectiveness, and interunit comparisons to those organization elite concerned with internal economy. If funds run short in equipment, a category transfer may have to be made from operating expenses at midyear.[r] A new division assigned a new and crucial task may be incurring unexpectedly heavy costs, which emphasize that drastic changes must be made in task accomplishment or a new strategy developed to seek a larger appropriation for the future. If the work performed by the new division serves as an input for other units in a situation of reciprocal interdependence, then the accounting information assumes even greater importance.

Far more study is needed by social scientists in this area that has been

[r]As noted previously, accounting systems have a political aspect, too, in that they communicate information to organizational polity and other interested actors in the policy subsystems—information that may be used for or against a public organization in a political sense, or by one faction or another internally.

considered so dry. Wildavsky has opened new vistas in looking at the budget process within a policy subsystem but has only hinted at its internal aspects.[33] Resource allocation is a compounded function of traditional rules, intergroup bargains, mechanics for deciding conflict, and elite perception of new areas for growth, change, or defense. We need far more studies of the accounting rules and budget process within public organizations, for this is a major aspect of internal economy.

Within the internal economy incentives are allocated to motivate performance. Those members of the organizational elite occupying roles in the structure of the internal economy allocate incentives like any other resource in line with their perceptions of tasks and how to efficiently accomplish them (and also in line with enhancing elite personal and political values). Allocational decisions are facilitated by accounting and forecasting mechanisms that summarize the current state of the organization, and by less formal, grapevine, information.

Somewhat different incentives are used to recruit and induce labor than to motivate continuing performance. Incentives may be monetary, nonmonetary (status, interpersonal), or symbolic. They vary not only in the "needs" they fulfil but in their delivery rate, tangibility, divisibility, and pervasiveness. Organizations will tend to have different stocks of incentives to draw on.

The Peace Corps obviously utilizes psychic incentives designed to appeal to youthful idealism (as well as desire for travel, and romanticism). These would be totally useless in the Post Office or the General Service Administration; the crisis-oriented paramilitary nature of Selective Service is conducive to use of such incentives as ceremonial presentation of longevity awards or director's appeals to patriotism; whereas the National Aeronautic and Space Administration is more likely to utilize professional peer group recognition as an incentive among scientists and engineers.

A major organizational change usually entails changes in the incentives that the cadre has available for allocation in efforts to induce effective task accomplishment. As the Strategic Air Command turned to missiles, the natural incentives built around flying came to be in short supply. In order to offset the loss of this incentive the command offered a variety of opportunities to "pick" one's next assignment or to pursue advanced degrees through correspondence courses while sitting in a missile silo in North Dakota.

Conclusion

Internal economy is an area given great attention by early PAT. In more recent times, as political scientists rushed to study the "politics" of bureaucracy, analysis of internal economy has been left to business administration, organizational sociologists studying the private sector, or to bureaus of public administration (viewed in departments of political science as community service agencies).

We contend that internal economy must be given more serious attention but in a broader perspective than used in early public administration. For no effort at building a theory of public administration can succeed without such attention.

Changes in the internal economy can be a major source of an internal polity struggle or can fundamentally alter an organization's relation to its environment. The conversion to computers and automatic data processing by a tax collection agency or a criminal investigation unit can suddenly throw the whole internal economy into turmoil, and eventually change internal and external polity relations. As the internal economy alters, it may provide an opportunity for a knowledgeable minority faction of the organization's elite to advance their power and prestige—perhaps with the help of influential in-contact others in the external political realm. Eventually a new dominant faction or coalition may emerge in the internal polity. In the examples mentioned above, that segment of the cadre commiteed to changing the internal economy, and with a knowledge of electronic data processing, may ascend to a position of cadre dominance; with the assistance perhaps of influential legislative committees, interest groups, or clientele users. There are many examples of the interplay between internal economy and other aspects of the organization, and it is this interplay we seek to highlight.

However, more is intended by the foregoing discussion than a mere alerting of the reader to the importance of internal political economy. Ultimately our thrust is to press for the development of propositions about the causes and consequences of differences among agencies along the crucial dimensions developed in this and the previous chapter. For instance, does a federated polity slow down the rate of systemwide change? Or does it, as James Q. Wilson suggests, facilitate the rate of *proposals* for change, while impeding the rate of *adoption* of change.[34] How does the level of required coordination among the units of an organization and the constitutional norms about the interrelations among units affect the degree of centralization of the internal polity? What are the conditions under which internal succession systems emerge, essentially limiting the choices of the nominally superior appointing officer? How do variations in accounting systems limit the surveillance of external actors? How do accounting systems shape perceptions of power and allocate resources to avoid accountability? How does the mode of funding interact with agency goals so as to displace agencies from pursuit of their original goals? These are the kinds of questions that a political economy approach brings together within one perspective.

Squaring the Circle? The Unification of Public Administration Theory

The greatest utility of the political-economy approach could be as a unifying force for a fractionated field (or fields?) of study. It may provide an opportunity to organize a multitude of discrete studies and phenomena in both public administration and organizational sociology that presently seem scattered and disconnected. It does, in fact, call for an organic union of public administration, political science, and organization theory-analysis. Hopefully, the strengths of each of these fields would be brought together in pursuit of a PAT. Organization analysis can provide a rigor and conceptual sophistication currently lacking in public administration; political science brings an awareness of political influences and environmental pressures upon public agencies (and organizations in general) that often seems slighted in organization theory and analysis, and public administration reminds us of the range of tasks and organizational problems of public agencies.

If ever a systematic and empirically based theory worthy of the name is to emerge, it must start with some unification of the diverse findings we have at hand, a merging of strengths across disciplinary lines, and a focusing of future research. Such unification and focus can be accomplished by a concentration on key dimensions (political and economic) that cut across or encompass both the internal and external aspects of public organizations. Furthermore, it is hoped that the proposed paradigm can provide explanatory leverage precisely where PAT has been so weak to date—on the processes of change in public organizations and the dynamics of organization-environment relations. It should be clear, however, that at this stage, the political economy approach is not even an accepted paradigm and certainly not a theory. Although some propositions and hypotheses have been advanced, the field is too large and complex for theoretical closure to be attempted.

Traditional Concerns of PAT

Many of public administration's traditional concerns need to be brought into a modern social science focus. In too many instances it has become identified with "practical" training, prescription, consulting work, normative writing, or pursuit of efficiency. None of these are necessarily inappropriate outcomes of objective social science analysis. But such "real life" concerns may be more likely to reach full potential with a paradigmatic focus and development of systematic empirical PAT.

The emergence of a behavioral focus in public administration (as represented by Herbert Simon) seems to have fallen short because it was focused on internal economy and a social psychological approach. Simon, Smithburg, and Thompson's text, though not intended as theory, came closer than anything else to date but, for reasons outlined earlier, also fell short. The field still awaits a broadly behavioral focus that encompasses all major dimensions of public organizations and that can lead to systematic and empirically based theory of administration in the public sector.

Each of the traditional concerns of public administration dealt with a key economic or political variable of public organizations, but did so in a piecemeal manner over decades, without any useful or conscious distinction between the political and economic, and always burdened with normative considerations. For example, Gulick and Urwick or Frederick Taylor and the scientific management school were concerned with structuring tasks for efficiency—an internal economy focus.[1] Similarly, students of budgeting, from the Taft commission down to developers of PPBS, have emphasized more heavily the surrogate market aspect of budgeting, that is, that budgeting is to save public funds by efficiency and economy. This has been functionally expressed as control of spending, management of activities, or currently both of these, plus planning. Not until quite recently has there been much departure from the shadow of a "surrogate market mechanism," nor an explicit sorting out of whether the "reforms" were having political or economic effects.[2]

Public administration has shown a similar nonfocused, largely normative, concern when it dealt with personnel administration. First, came the great civil service reform, then the development of techniques of personnel administration and a little scientific management under a central control agency. And now there is in progress an effort to decentralize personnel matters and explore ways of enhancing the status and motivation of civil servants. Again, students of public administration dealt with a vital factor in the political economy of public organizations (the handling of a major factor of production, personnel) but did so as participants in a crusade, not as analysts. Accordingly, the political and economic aspects were never differentiated, and the organizational consequences were underanalyzed.

This is evident when a leading student of personnel administration can review its history of "reforms" in America and conclude "the net result has been disappointing. . . . Indeed, some observers believe we have failed to achieve a first-class public service *because* of these reforms. . . ."[3] The remark is more like that of a participant than of a detached observer; and it is an incredible admission that, unfortunately, could have just as well been uttered by a student of almost any other concern of public administration. We have outgrown the false dichotomy between politics and administration but are still far short of viewing the various phenomena and traditional concerns of the public administration field as phenomena to be studied as detached observers. We may try to be objective, but we still view these concerns as action-participants do, as matters for direct participation and intervention to assure a certain outcome.

What is perhaps most lacking is a focus upon an empirical entity—the public organization or program: a key agent in the formulation and execution of policy; at the center of a particular policy subsystem; having greater symbolic significance than any equivalent private entity; and whose funding and goal setting processes are largely externally controlled and often subject to political struggle. The development of an empirical stance depends upon our ability to focus upon this entity and to view our traditional concerns as phenomena that impinge upon it politically or economically and thus affect its behavior.

Comparative Developmental Administration

Though our ways of treating our subject have yet to show much change, a concern for reform is no longer as openly fashionable among American students of public administration as it was, or it has taken different forms.[a] Still, these same traditional reformist concerns are current and vital matters in the so-called "developing administrative. systems," whether they be traditional, autocratic, revolutionary, authoritarian, communist, military, or some other form. They should continue to be the concern of public administration, especially in developmental and comparative subfields. But our traditional concerns with budgeting, civil service reform, efficiency need to be approached in a broader and nonnormative way. If one views developmental administration nonnormatively, the distinction between efficiency-oriented reforms and political considerations resembles the distinction the framework makes between political and economic. If so, then the political-economy paradigm has a range of utility beyond the American scene. With the political-economy approach, the struggle between "efficiency reform" and "politics" that is taking place in developing systems can be studied in a detached manner.

The "reforms" or changes in developing systems often do not have the results their advocates suggest, but they do have significant impact that deserves study. The inception of a civil service system often has significant consequences for an organization's internal economy by protecting or buffering the technical core and regulating the competence and turnover of the labor force. Instituting an executive budget may make drastic alterations in the external, political aspects of a public organization by throwing it into intense new competition or bringing it under unfriendly dominance of a central budget office.

---

[a]See Frank Marini, TOWARD A NEW PUBLIC ADMINISTRATION: THE MINNOW-BROOK PERSPECTIVE (Scranton, Pa.: Chandler Publishing, 1971), passim. It can be argued that in some ways the "new public administration" is much more traditional than new. New faces have joined the ranks, some new concerns have arisen in line with changed times, and a few new ways of expressing those concerns appeared, but basically the "new" is very traditional in its prescriptive and interventionist proclivities.

On the other hand, many seemingly "regressive" steps that lack a "good government" appearance are nonetheless aimed at more effective task accomplishment. Militarizing of a sluggish civilian bureaucracy may be an effort to bring about effective task accomplishment in order to avert a decline in a regime's legitimacy. Placing high proportions of indigenous non-experts in the administrative hierarchy of an economic development program may be an effort to mobilize people politically and establish legitimacy, both of which are believed by those in power to be more important than efficient task accomplishment in a narrower sense. And distributing "civil service jobs" in careful proportions to persons with certain tribal backgrounds may be more important to the survival and to effective task accomplishment of a public organization in Ghana or Nigeria than adherence to strict achievement and efficiency criteria.

A similar example can be drawn from the recent history of organizations in the Soviet Union. Vernon Aspaturian details how the Soviet Foreign Ministry went through a series of changes which replaced fiery but "unwashed" bolshevik ideologists with pragmatic, professional diplomats, including a few who had formerly served in the Czarist diplomatic corps.[4] And Khrushchev in 1962 split the party central committees of oblasts into groups specializing in agriculture and those specializing in industrialization—a response to a need for more professionalism and task accomplishment rather than legitimacy and ideology. In November 1964, as a part of Khrushchev's ouster, the decision was reversed—perhaps as a part of a payoff to national central committee members who had never liked the diminution of status for oblast chairmen, and who consequently supported Khrushchev's opponents.[5] In both the "reform" and "counterreform," political economy variables were clearly at work. The framework can provide the insights needed to understand the consequences of these "reforms," or what may appear to be "counterreforms," for developing administrative systems. All public administrative systems can be seen through the lens of political economy as being struggles to balance legitimacy, over-all directions, and major economic dimensions, on the one hand, with, distribution of resources and coordination for effective task accomplishment, on the other.

Whether students of comparative and developmental administration take the stance of interventionist participants or of detached academic observers their analyses might profit by use of the proposed paradigm. Currently the more detached academic observers tend to utilize variations of the Weberian rational bureaucratic model, and discuss the interplay, overlap, and conflict between that structure and traditional and changing societies.[b] This approach has a utility, but it is greatest at a macro-systemic level. As comparative development administration is further refined, it will be desirable to move beyond the macro-systemic

---

[b]Fred W. Riggs, ADMINISTRATION IN DEVELOPING COUNTRIES (Boston: Houghton Mifflin, 1964). We recognize we are making an exaggerated, hard and fast distinction between "detached academic observers" and "action-participant analysts." (Riggs, for instance, has been heavily involved in consulting work.) Nonetheless, we think there is a very real difference in stance.

level of analysis typical to date[c] to the more finite and ultimately more useful level of public organizations and policy subsystems. We feel the political-economy approach yields additional analytic results without losing any of the important insights of the macro approach. Although it has not been demonstrated here, we believe the political-economy approach, with its focus on constitutional normative orders and its openness to the environment, can handle the impact of different cultures and societal structures on public organizations.

Policy Analysis

The proposed paradigm could give PAT a significant part in developing the important area of concern within political science called "policy analysis." Recent efforts in this area have focused on systemic inputs and outputs. It is not certain whether this is because political scientists are currently enraptured with only the quantifiable or because they lack the requisite tools for institutional analysis. Probably both. What is certain, however, is that the discipline is a long way from being able to explain why certain policies take the particular patterns they assume.

Thomas Dye's study of policy outputs in the states of the union points up the murkiness of the area that analysis must penetrate if we are to understand the phenomenon we call "policy."[6] Dye's work implicitly calls for the application of an analytic tool like our framework. He shows a high correlation between economic development of a state and the level of policy outputs in selected subject areas, but a low correlation between policy outcomes and such political variables as level of interparty competition, voter participation, degree of malapportionment, and division of two-party control. Thus, "political" variables seem to have little bearing on policy outcomes.[d]

---

[c]There is an important conceptual strand in comparative developmental public administration that in several respects resembles the political-economy approach. We refer to John Dorsey's "An Information-Energy Model," in PAPERS AND COMPARATIVE PUBLIC ADMINISTRATION, eds. Ferrel Heady and Sybil Stokes (Ann Arbor: Institute of Public Administration, University of Michigan, 1962). Dorsey's approach is adaptable to macro- or micro-level analysis. It is definitely ecological and focuses on the interrelationship between the internal functioning of an organization and gross environmental changes. It is also nonnormative and nonprescriptive. We will not undertake a discussion of what shortcomings, if any, this model has. Perhaps it is merely cast in such an original mold of thinking that most students have difficulty utilizing it. If a model is to serve a paradigmatic function it must utilize concepts common and familiar to students of a subject and it must be developed to a level that facilitates adaptation.

[d]Dye, of course, has been criticized on several grounds. Ira Sharkansky says, "Dye's argument is persuasive but tends to be exaggerated. A close examination of his statistics reveals their weaknesses. Of the 356 separate measures of association between an economic and a policy measure that he reports in his book, only 16 (4 percent) are strong enough to indicate that an economic trait accounts for even half of the interstate differences in policy." Sharkansky, POLICY ANALYSIS IN POLITICAL SCIENCE, (Chicago: Markham,

But rather than showing that politics is unimportant in policy, Dye's results show how myopic we have been in defining "politics." The interplay in policymaking between a public organization, its competitors, superiors, clientele, interest groups, and legislative committees is just as "political" as parties and voter participation.

Policy is made at the nexus of politics and economics. Specifically it is formulated and/or executed by public organizations imbedded in policy subsystems, each with their own matrix of pressures and cross-pressures. It is probable that economic development provides a *resource backdrop for the perceptions* of constraints and opportunities by policy elites (especially the cadres of public organizations), organizational routines and procedures, elite competition, role perception, available technologies, and a variety of other matters we have touched on in this essay.

Dye and most other students of public policy do not purport to penetrate this realm nor explain how policy is made. The importance of general economic environment upon policy process and outcome is apparent. But until there is a conscious broadening of what is called political, and an extension of our concerns into the realm of public organizations and policy subsystems, policy analysis will remain an enterprise of limited productivity.

The Paradigm and Democratic Theory

The other area of concern in which the framework may be able to make a contribution is in the realm of democratic theory. Pluralism (or plural elitism), which is currently the "dominant image" of the American political system, requires still further refinement. Specifically, refinement should entail (1) an effort to identify shifts in plural elite configurations as issues or perceptions of them change in different policy arenas and (2) development of an understanding of how the behavior of institutional actors affects policy outcomes, with that behavior being the result of political and economic influences. Theodore Lowi's

---

1970), p. 8. The greatest problems with the work of Dye and others lies in what their works have *not* done, rather than what they have done. Rather than criticize what has not been done, let us merely agree with Robert Salisbury and John Heinz that the work has not dealt with policies not cast in the form of expenditures—"which make or revise rules, establish or disestablish structures and programs and administer justice"—and left a gap of major theoretical importance concerning why political decision-makers act as they do. See the Robert H. Salisbury and John Heinz article, "A Theory of Policy Analysis: And Some Preliminary Applications," in Sharkansky, ibid., p. 40. A recent addition to the literature which runs counter to the dominant theme is Brian R. Fry and Richard F. Winters, "The Politics of Redistribution," AMERICAN POLITICAL SCIENCE REVIEW 64, no. 2 (June 1970): 508. At the 1970 sessions of the Southern Political Science convention both Dye and Sharkansky presented papers that sought to deal with the criticisms leveled against the work of Dye—thus, in effect, admitting the validity of the criticisms and moving to handle them. For a full citation on recent empirical policy analysis, see fn. 1, p. 59, in the Sharkansky work cited above.

essay, "American Business, Public Policy, Case-Studies and Political Theory" is an excellent partial step toward identifying changing patterns of elite configuration.[7] As noted earlier, Lowi suggests that elite configurations are related to the type of policy that is the subject of conflict: distributive, regulative, or redistributive. Clearly this is a step in the right direction. But such conceptualization can be enriched by greater emphasis upon the role of "the agency." *Policy is as much, or more, a product of factors within the interstices of the system's "black box"—the conversion process—as it is of pressures or inputs from outside.* Virtually all policies are heavily influenced by public organizations in formulation as well as execution.

But we are saying more than "look at bureaucracy—it is important in policymaking!" Others have said that and said it better. Rather, we are saying that democratic theory seeks to answer the question of who is behind certain policy and government action and the answer in many cases is—an organization or organizational process; not a power elite, voters, or a man, but an organization. The outcome is decidedly different emanating from a collection of humans in an organization than it is from any of the other sources.

One of the most powerful presentations of this conceptual approach is found in Graham Allison's analysis of the 1962 Cuban missile crisis.[8] The crisis came into being when an American U-2 photographed Soviet ballistic missile bases being established in Cuba. President Kennedy responded by declaring "strict quarantine of all offensive military equipment under shipment to Cuba," and demanding the elimination of the bases.[9] After several days of high-pressure planning the United States chose the policy of establishing a naval blockade to which the Soviets finally responded by ceasing exportation of missiles and the dismantling of the bases. Allison analyzes the crisis using three different models: "rational policy, organizational process, and bureaucratic politics."[e] He convincingly demonstrates that the last two are far richer in analytical power than the first.

In the crisis policy emerged from organizations and organization processes. Thus the timing of the discovery of the missiles was crucial in determining the kinds of options open to the United States. That timing was a result of set organizational processes of the CIA and the air force as well as a struggle between them for jurisdiction over U-2 flights. A blockade was finally picked as the major option, rather than a surgical air strike, but that decision did not grow out of some "higher" rationality or national interest but out of air force strategic planning processes and existing repertoires which defined the Soviet

---

[e]Allison, "Conceptual Models and the Cuban Missile Crisis," AMERICAN POLITICAL SCIENCE REVIEW 62 (September 1969): 690. Note, we recognize the problem implicated in the term "rational." It is Allison's choice not ours. By it he means an analyst using a rational policy model "attempts to understand happenings as the more or less purposive acts of unified national government. He is, of course, applying it to foreign policy analysis. We think what he has to say has meaning for policy analysis in general and indeed for the entire development of political science.

missiles as "mobile." To the air force the "mobile" classification called for such a huge air strike on collateral targets that it might endanger Russian technicians and appear as a prelude to invasion. And the navy adhered rigidly to its repertoires and SOPs in conducting the blockade, despite their conflict with the most explicit and contrary presidential orders on certain points.

Policy was also a result of a variety of political games that were being played by participants. President Kennedy was involved in the game of national congressional elections. He had responded hawkishly to criticism that his Cuban policies were soft on communism. The criticisms and his responses left him with little option but a strong response to the missiles. The Joint Chiefs of Staff were playing in a micro game in which they saw the missile crisis as an opportunity to recoup status lost at the Bay of Pigs. The CIA also urged strong measures because their original warnings about missiles had been ignored. Secretary of Defense Robert McNamara, on the other hand, was playing out a role he had created for himself and the office of secretary of defense, in which he acted as a cool restraint upon the military. Accordingly, he urged a more moderate course. That his reputation was so high in the Cabinet at that time and that his department "had the action" were powerful forces working in favor of his position. When he was joined by Senator Robert Kennedy and speechwriter Theodore Sorenson, who both played roles of "watchdogs for the President's place in history," the initially favored air strike was abandoned for the more moderate blockade.

Allison's "rational policy model," which sees the nation or government as "a rational, unitary decision-maker," is prevalent in writings on international relations and foreign policy and has no direct equivalent in democratic theory.[10] But all democratic theory takes somewhat the same stance. That is, theorists, whether classical democratic, power elitist, or plural elitist, all assume a logical means-ends relationship in policy that the theorist believes serves the interest of the larger society or some group's interest. Just as the foreign policy analyst assumes that given the options of a situation and what he perceives the nation's strategic objectives to be, a nation has only one policy option that "rationally" serves its interest; so the democratic theorist assumes that given the pattern of power in society, the interests of certain groups, or what he perceives to be the "best" interests of society as a whole, a "rational" policy option will emerge, one which either serves a means-end logic or a group self-interest. For a classical democratic theorist a policy outcome would be explained by turning to expressions of majority will (or failures of officials to adhere to the same); for a power elitist it would be explained by ascertaining the interlocking interests of that group and their strategic location in the policy process; for a plural elitist, an explanation would lie in the residual outcome of a clash of pluralistic interest groups.

As the currently dominant image in American political science, plural elitism sees policy as the outcome of competing interest-group pressures with occasional mass influence through the election process. Implicitly, the public interest is supposed to emerge as if guided by an invisible hand from the competition of elites outside government; however, if democratic theory remains dominated by this model, our picture of how the American (and other) political systems operate will be seriously deficient. If we are to ascertain how policy is made, and by whom, we must look in the right places. For a variety of reasons we have failed to look in the institutional intersticies of governments, in the structure and processes of public organizations. As Allison says in speaking of the organization process model,

A "government" consists of a conglomerate of semifeudal, loosely allied organizations, each with a substantial life of its own, . . . governments perceive problems through organizational sensors, . . . define alternatives and estimate consequences as organizations process information, . . . (and governments) act as their organizations enact routines.[11]

Government behavior can be understood largely as "outputs of large organizations functioning according to standard patterns of behavior"—within quasi-independent domains.[12] Or alternately, the bureaucratic politics model reveals national behavior as "outcomes of intricate and subtle, simultaneous, overlapping games among players located in *positions*"; positions that define what they "may and must do," the "advantages and handicaps" with which each can "enter and play in various games," and the "cluster of obligations for the performance of certain tasks."[13]

Both the organization process and bureaucratic politics model may be vital missing links in policy analysis and in democratic theorists' efforts to flesh out their picture of how the system operates.[f] Using these models the answer to the democratic theorists' question "Who's running this place?" may be considerably more complex and subtle than the ones developed up to now.

Allison's use of the imagery of a chess game may be illustrative.[14] Up to now democratic theory has seen government as a chess game with pieces moved by "outside forces"—i.e., "the people," "the power elite," or a squabbling team of plural elites or interest groups. Perhaps we need to think of pieces moving as a result of "internal forces." It is as though, for instance, each piece has a set of wheels, internal motor, sensory devices, miniature computer, and guidance system, which means that it is sometimes moved by outside forces and sometimes in response to its own reading of its environment and its internal dynamics. Imagine also that although the individual piece "reads" its environ-

---

[f]It is interesting to note the "conversion" to the bureaucratic politics school of a famous academician and practitioner, the irrepressible Daniel P. Moynihan. In the preface to the second edition of his book MAXIMUM FEASIBLE MISUNDERSTANDING, he says that the only weakness in his much criticized book was that it "almost entirely ignored the *bureaucratic* component of events" and that he "paid too little heed to other actors on the same scene who were not less political, but whose politics were those of a bureaucracy." (New York: Free Press, 1970, pp. 27 and 28.)

ment and acts accordingly, its ability to "read" and its repertory of responses are limited, and they are conditioned upon the basis of political and economic factors. Each one is programed by these factors. The State Department moves as it does because of the way it as an organization sees itself constrained or presented with opportunities. The Strategic Air Command perceives and moves in still another way, and the Office of Education within the Department of Health, Education, and Welfare may respond as it does because an outside player "overrides" its internal machinery and program.[15]

Or to carry things further, imagine all the above conditions *plus* the fact that we, the observers, can see only one game board while in fact each piece is playing in *several* other games that we are unable to see; imagine further that the game boards are not square with one another but overlap in a variety of ways. Accordingly, the self-directed piece we can see is, unbeknownst to us, moving in several games at once, playing out strategies dictated by differing locations on each game board—a lower right corner on one, the center of the board on another, the upper left on still another.

Public organizations are not merely important actors in a policy process. Sometimes organizations as total entities, not the men at the top of the organization chart, are *the* makers of policy. The organization's goals, myths, processes, procedures, or domain consciousness in effect "make" policy. Much of our foreign policy is an outcome of the State Department as an organizational entity regardless of the efforts at policy direction by any president, secretary of state, Congress, or any other actor. The course of the Viet Nam War and the disastrous focus on "search and destroy tactics" rather than on "clear and hold" operations consistent with counterinsurgency warfare was largely a result of the army's organizational response to suddenly expanded combat operations. The deaths of Kent and Jackson State students were in large part the outcome of the organizational responses of the Ohio National Guard and the Mississippi State Police. The answer to the question "Who's running this place?" may often be distressing but accurate answers such as "institutional inertia," "a certain organization process," or a particular political economy configuration for a public organization.

It will come as no surprise to the reader that we feel the political-economy framework can play an important part in bringing Allison's organization process and bureaucratic politics model to bear on the questions of democratic theory and in analyzing the internal forces of the "chess game" of government. The approach holds out the possibility of transforming the phrase "bureaucratic politics" from an epithet to an analytic tool.

If one would understand why American conscription policies have taken the particular form they have since 1964, he will find preciously little enlightenment if he tries to find "public opinion" affecting legislators, or if he tries to unearth the machinations of a power elite, and scarcely much more if he seeks to explain them by reference to shifting interest groups or plural elites. For example, public opinion in the late 1960s grew increasingly negative to the operation of Selective Service and finally to conscription itself, but Congress for a long time refused to make any changes whatsoever; and the interest group configuration surrounding the draft had been stable since at least 1945. It was a segment of the power elite, the "Pentagon," which first "turned over the rock" by initiating a study of the draft and "leaking" unfavorable results.

The answers to the "what" and "by whom" of conscription policy lie in the political economy of the Selective Service System. More concretely, they lie in the following factors: (1) perceptions by organizational cadre of external political pressures which led the system to build up rigid defenses and alliances with interest groups and congressional committees; (2) the pressures of two inexorable external economic factors—excess manpower, which pushed the system to increasingly vulnerable deferment decisions in an effort to look like it was "using" all the manpower, and the Vietnam war, which meant that many of the recipients of these "vulnerable" or questionable decisions lived normal lives while others inducted on equally questionable grounds died; (3) an internal polity completely dominated by a charismatic leader, which meant that alternative means of coping with growing crises were never available; and (4) an internal economy fortified (or ossified) by closed systems of recruiting and socializing cadre, and centered on task accomplishment by local boards which were believed (erroneously) to shield the system against external political attacks. In these political-economy factors lie the explanations for the moves of the particular chess piece called "Selective Service."[16]

Because the chess pieces often move according to their own political-economy "programs" or their own readings of political and economic environmental factors, the analytical direction being suggested for democratic theory is clear, as is the tool for the type of analysis required. We also note Allison's rhetorical query:

Can the organization process model be modified, to suggest where change is likely? Attention to organization change should afford greater understanding of why particular programs and SOP's are maintained by identifiable types of organizations.[17]

Again we see it as a specific call for an instrument of analysis like the political-economy framework. It is geared to suggest where change is likely to occur; and to proceed to fill in the details on why certain types of organizations maintain particular programs and standard operating procedures. We have suggested that the political-economy framework can serve as a serious step toward developing a systematic empirical theory of public administration: one that tries to draw both traditional concerns of public administration and more recent ones back into the fold of political science; seeks to find a place for more normative concerns as a spin-off of empirical theory-building, rather than rejecting such concerns as somehow improper; and makes significant contributions to the development of other subject-matter areas in political science and organizational sociology. Admittedly that is suggesting a lot. If we have "bitten off" more than the proposed paradigm can "chew," may we suggest a "fall back position"? The further development and application of the political-economy approach would surely have to be counted as valuable if it contributed to just *one* of the many problems we hope to see it handle.

Notes

Notes

Chapter 1
A Fragmented Field in Need of Theory

1. Karl Deutsch, THE NERVES OF GOVERNMENT, chap. 1. On the roles of models and theory see George J. Graham, Jr., METHODOLOGICAL FOUNDATIONS FOR POLITICAL ANALYSIS (Lexington: Ginn-Xerox, 1972). Chap. 6 discusses the nuances of forms of theory and paradigms and how they relate to empirical generalizations.

2. Thomas S. Kuhn, "The Structure of Scientific Revolutions," INTERNATIONAL ENCYCLOPEDIA OF UNITED SCIENCES, vol. 2, no. 2 (Chicago, 1962), chap. 2. Martin Landau has applied Kuhn's notions to the state of research on formal organizations. Martin Landau, "Sociology and the Study of Formal Organizations," Comparative Administration Group of the American Society for Public Administration, Special Series No. 8 (Washington, D.C., 1966), p. 38.

3. Landau, ibid.

4. See Philip S. Kronenberg, "The Scientific and Moral Authority of Empirical Theory of Public Administration," in TOWARD A NEW PUBLIC ADMINISTRATION: THE MINNOWBROOK PERSPECTIVE, ed. Frank Marini (Scranton, Pa.: Chandler Publishing, 1971), chap. 7.

5. For a good example of an effort at settling the boundary problem and providing some unity see Dwight Waldo, "Scope of the Theory of Public Administration," in THEORY AND PRACTICE OF PUBLIC ADMINISTRATION: SCOPE, OBJECTIVES, AND METHODS, American Academy of Political and Social Science (Philadelphia, 1968). It is also a good example of loose use of the word "theory" and eclecticism, as Waldo concludes with yet another list of special subject-matter concerns.

6. See R.A. Dahl and C.E. Lindblom, POLITICS, ECONOMICS AND WELFARE (New York: Harper & Row, 1953), chap. 1. They also emphasize that all forms of government and related economies are a means of social control. In any one situation a particular politicoeconomic means of social control will be more "rational," "effective," or "functional" than another.

7. Ibid., p. 456.

8. Ibid., pp. 458-64.

9. Murray Edelman, SYMBOLIC USES OF POLITICS (Urbana: University of Illinois Press, 1967), pp. 5, 56, 74. See also Harold Lasswell, PSYCHOPATHOLOGY AND POLITICS (Chicago: University of Chicago Press, 1930), pp. 75-76.

10. Edelman, ibid., p. 5 (italics added).

11. Dwight Waldo, THE STUDY OF PUBLIC ADMINISTRATION (New York: Random House, 1955), p. 9.

12. Herbert Simon, Donald Smithburg, and Victor Thompson, PUBLIC ADMINISTRATION (New York: Alfred A. Knopf, 1950).

13. William Mitchell, PUBLIC CHOICE IN AMERICA (Chicago: Markham, 1971), 85-88.

14. This is a very oversimplified treatment of economists' definition of public goods. For two relevant sources see Carl S. Shoup, PUBLIC FINANCE (New York: Aldine Publishing Co., 1969), chaps. 4-7. And Mancur Olson, Jr., THE LOGIC OF COLLECTIVE ACTION: PUBLIC GOODS AND THE THEORY OF GROUPS (Cambridge, Mass.: Harvard University Press, 1965).

15. Benjamin Walter, "On Contrasts Between Private Firms and Governmental Bureaus," in POWER IN ORGANIZATIONS, ed. Mayer Zald (Nashville, Tenn.: Vanderbilt University Press, 1970), p. 323.

16. Ibid.

17. In "scientific" political science, concerns with policy have been looked at askance until recently. Charles Lindblom's, THE POLICY-MAKING PROCESS (Englewood Cliffs, N.J.: Prentice-Hall, 1968), is a concise review and synthesis of a renewed behavioral interest in policy making. And a spate of readers attempting to focus on the policy process have emerged. See Austen Ranney, ed., POLITICAL SCIENCE AND PUBLIC POLICY (Chicago: Markham, 1969); and Ira Sharkansky, ed., POLICY ANALYSIS IN POLITICAL SCIENCE (Chicago: Markham, 1970). One of the best of these readers and one that is conceptually closest to our perspective is Fremont J. Lyden, George Shipman, and Morton Kroll, eds., POLICIES, DECISIONS AND ORGANIZATION (New York: Appleton-Century-Crofts, 1969). The best known perhaps is Thomas Dye's POLITICS, ECONOMICS AND THE PUBLIC; POLICY OUTCOMES IN THE AMERICAN STATES (Chicago: Rand McNally, 1966). For a citation of these empirically oriented works, see n. 1, p. 59, of the Sharkansky reader.

18. Lyden, ibid.

19. Roger Hilsman, TO MOVE A NATION (New York: Dell Publishing, 1968), p. 17.

20. Ibid., p. 18. See also Harold Seidman, who, after 25 years in the Bureau of Budget, said, "The basic issues of federal organization and administration relate to power: who shall control it and to what ends?", POLITICS, POSITION AND POWER (New York: Oxford University Press, 1970), p. 27.

21. The discussion here is extremely selective and is not intended to be a thorough history of either public administration or organizational sociology. For a good treatment of the former see Alan Altshuler, "The Study of Public Administration," in THE POLITICS OF FEDERAL BUREAUCRACY, ed. Altshuler (New York: Dodd, Mead, 1968), pp. 55-72. For a partial treatment of the latter see Nicos P. Mouzelis, ORGANIZATION AND BUREAUCRACY: AN ANALYSIS OF MODERN THEORIES (Chicago: Aldine, 1968).

22. As Dwight Waldo says, "organization theory is often used to designate a focus of interest in research, theorizing, and professional writing. It represents

convenience, not rigor. Dwight Waldo, Martin Landau et al., "The Study of Organizational Behavior: Status, Problems and Trends," American Society for Public Administration, Comparative Administration Group Series, no. 8 (Washington, D.C., 1966), p. 2.

23. Gulick and Urwick, eds., PAPERS ON THE SCIENCE OF ADMINISTRATION (New York: Columbia University, Institute of Public Administration, 1937); or Frederick W. Taylor, SCIENTIFIC MANAGEMENT (New York: Harper & Row, 1971).

24. Simon, Smithburg, and Thompson, PUBLIC ADMINISTRATION.

25. See for example, chapter headings such as "Securing Teamwork: The Structure of Authority and Status," "Securing Teamwork: The Organization of Communication," "Tactics of Execution: Securing Compliance," "Tactics of Execution: Reducing the Cost of Change," "Selection of the Team: Personnel Processes."

26. Landau, "Study of Organizational Behavior," p. 43. For a discussion of the paradigmatic problem, see Herbert Storing, "The Science of Administration," in ESSAYS ON THE SCIENTIFIC STUDY OF POLITICS, ed. Herbert Storing (New York: Holt, Rinehart & Winston, 1962).

27. Simon et al., PUBLIC ADMINISTRATION, p. 8.

28. Dwight Waldo, COMPARATIVE PUBLIC ADMINISTRATION: PROLOGUE, PROBLEMS AND PROMISES. American Society for Public Administration, Comparative Administration Group Series, no. 2 (Washington, D.C., 1964), p. 27.

29. There are a number of contributors to the literature of organizational analysis. Prominent among them and clearly representing an intellectual strand upon which we have drawn are the works of Philip Selznick and his students. For Selznick, see TVA AND THE GRASS ROOTS (hardback, Berkeley: University of California Press, 1949); LEADERSHIP IN ADMINISTRATION (Evanston, Ill., 1957); and his "Foundations of the Theory of Organizations," AMERICAN SOCIOLOGICAL REVIEW 13 (1948). Students of Selznick who have taken a similar approach are Charles Perrow in his earlier works such as "The Analysis of Goals in Complex Organizations," AMERICAN SOCIOLOGICAL REVIEW 26 (1961); and Burton Clark, OPEN-DOOR COLLEGE (New York: McGraw-Hill, 1960). Representative of other "strands" are the works of Alvin Gouldner and Peter Blau and their students.

30. Shoup, PUBLIC FINANCE, pp. 102-103.

31. Rourke, BUREAUCRACY, POLITICS AND PUBLIC POLICY, (Boston: Little, Brown, 1969), especially chaps. 2, 3, and 4. Ultimately it may be useful to borrow the terminology and models of conflict or strategy of theorists to highlight the external bargaining, conflict, and coalitional behavior of organizations. See Thomas C. Schelling, THE STRATEGY OF CONFLICT (New York: Oxford University Press, 1963).

32. The concept of an organizational constitution is discussed in Zald, "Political Economy: A Framework for Comparative Analysis," in POWER IN

ORGANIZATIONS, ed. M.N. Zald (Nashville, Tenn.: Vanderbilt University Press, 1970), pp. 221-61.

Chapter 2
The Environment of Agencies

1. For a discussion of precarious values, see Burton Clark, "Organizational Adaptation and Precarious Values," AMERICAN SOCIOLOGICAL REVIEW 21 (1956): 327-36.

2. Rourke, BUREAUCRACY, POLITICS AND PUBLIC POLICY, chaps. 2-4.

3. Burton Clark, "Organizational Adaptation," pp. 327-36.

4. David Truman, POLITICS AND GOVERNMENT IN THE UNITED STATES, 2d ed. (New York: Harcourt, Brace and World, 1968), chap. 14. Also Rourke, BUREAUCRACY, POLITICS AND PUBLIC POLICY, chap. 2, and Simon et al., PUBLIC ADMINISTRATION, chap. 19.

5. Truman, POLITICS, chap. 14.

6. Gary L. Wamsley, SELECTIVE SERVICE AND A CHANGING AMERICA (Columbus, O.: Chas. E. Merrill Co., 1969), chap. 7.

7. For a good example of the extraordinary efforts necessary to bring about the changes in the government agencies involved in the policy issues on tobacco so that danger warnings could appear on cigarettes see Lee J. Fritschler, SMOKING AND POLITICS (New York: Appleton-Century-Crofts, 1969).

8. Ira Sharkansky, "Four Agencies and an Appropriations Subcommittee: A Comparative Study of Budget Strategies," MIDWEST JOURNAL OF POLITICAL SCIENCE 9, no. 3 (August 1965): 254-81, and "An Appropriations Subcommittee and Its Client Agencies: A Comparative Study of Supervision and Control," AMERICAN POLITICAL SCIENCE REVIEW 59, no. 3 (September 1965): 622-28.

9. Randall B. Ripley, ed., PUBLIC POLICIES AND THEIR POLITICS (New York: W.W. Norton, 1966), p. 29.

10. L. John Roos, Master's thesis, University of Chicago, 1968, in Theodore J. Lowi, THE END OF LIBERALISM: IDEOLOGY, POLICY, AND THE CRISIS OF PUBLIC AUTHORITY (New York: W.W. Norton, 1969), p. 208.

11. Daniel Willick, "Political Goals and the Structure of Government Bureaus," paper delivered at American Sociological Association, Washington, D.C., 1970.

12. Sol Levine and Paul E. White, "Exchange as a Conceptual Framework for the Study of Interorganizational Relationships," ADMINISTRATIVE SCIENCE QUARTERLY 5 (March 1957): 583-601.

13. Such a depiction of events gained wide currency among political commentators in 1970. For rather solid substantiation of it see the transcript of

NBC's COMMENT, 24 January 1970, which contains interviews with Leon Panetta, fired director of the Office of Civil Rights for HEW, and James Farmer, who resigned as assistant secretary for Health, Education, and Welfare. See also L.E. Panetta and P. Gall, BRING US TOGETHER: THE NIXON TEAM AND CIVIL RIGHTS RETREAT (New York: Lippincott, 1971).

14. Participant observation, Wamsley, 1964.

15. Aaron Wildavsky, THE POLITICS OF THE BUDGETARY PROCESS (Boston: Little, Brown, 1964), pp. 27, 172.

16. Wildavsky, ibid., p. 66.

17. Wildavsky, ibid., p. 173.

18. Truman, POLITICS AND GOVERNMENT, pp. 457-567.

19. See testimony of Gary L. Wamsley, "The Selective Service System: Its Operation, Practices, and Procedures," HEARINGS BEFORE THE SUBCOMMITTEE ON ADMINISTRATIVE PRACTICE AND PROCEDURE OF THE COMMITTEE ON THE JUDICIARY, U.S., Senate, 91st Cong., 1st Sess. (Washington, D.C.: U.S. Government Printing Office, 1969), pp. 181-222.

20. Wamsley, SELECTIVE SERVICE AND A CHANGING AMERICA, p. 214. Rooney's influence over State Department has become legendary among those close to the department (discussion with Charles Frankel, former assistant secretary of state). See also Aaron Wildavsky, THE POLITICS OF THE BUDGETARY PROCESS (Boston: Little, Brown, 1964), passim. River's influence scarcely needs documentation. See Robert G. Sherrill, "King of the Military Mountain," THE NATION, 19 January 1970, pp. 40-47.

21. The importance of perceptions and roles cannot be overemphasized. See Wildavsky, THE POLITICS OF THE BUDGETARY PROCESS; also Thomas J. Anton, THE POLITICS OF STATE EXPENDITURE IN ILLINOIS (Urbana: University of Illinois Press, 1963) and Richard J. Fenno, Jr., THE POWER OF THE PURSE (Boston: Little, Brown, 1966).

22. Jesse Burkhead, GOVERNMENT BUDGETING (New York: John Wiley and Sons, 1956), p. 87.

23. Wildavsky, "Political Implications of Budgetary Reform," PUBLIC ADMINISTRATION REVIEW 21 (Autumn 1961): 183-90; "The Political Economy of Efficiency, Cost Benefit Analysis, Systems Analysis and Program Budgeting," PUBLIC ADMINISTRATION REVIEW 26 (1966), pp. 292-310.

24. Anthony Downs, INSIDE BUREAUCRACY (Boston: Little, Brown), p. 44.

25. For numerous excellent examples see Anton, POLITICS OF STATE EXPENDITURE, pp. 46-47, 69-70, 203-204.

26. Shoup, PUBLIC FINANCE, p. 105.

27. Though he does not confine his conceptualization to public organizations, the ideas of Charles Perrow are very useful in this regard. See his "A Framework for the Comparative Analysis of Organizations," AMERICAN SOCIOLOGICAL REVIEW 26 (1961).

28. G.L. Wamsley, "The Joint Chiefs of Staff: An Organizational Analysis," paper, Graduate School of Public and International Affairs, University of Pittsburgh, 1965.

There have been some changes in the national security policy process that make the above analysis a bit dated. For an account of changes see Keith Clark and Laurence Legere, THE PRESIDENT AND THE MANAGEMENT OF NATIONAL SECURITY (New York: Praeger, 1969) and Lawrence J. Korb, "The Secretary of Defense and the Joint Chiefs of Staff: The Relationship in the Budgetary Process, 1947-1971," paper delivered at the 1971 Conference of the Inter-University Seminar on the Armed Forces and Society, Chicago (1971).

29. See Aaron Wildavsky, "Political Economy of Efficiency," pp. 292-310.

Chapter 3
The Internal Political Economy

1. Herbert Simon, ADMINISTRATIVE BEHAVIOR (New York: Free Press, 1965), p. 118.

2. See Zald, "Political Economy: A Comparative Approach . . . ," for an analysis of the relationship of polity forms to major "constitutional" differences in the bases of organizations.

3. Selznick, TVA AND THE GRASS ROOTS (paperback, New York: Harper & Row, 1966), p. 259; or see his LEADERSHIP IN ADMINISTRATION.

4. Selznick, TVA and LEADERSHIP.

5. Selznick, TVA and LEADERSHIP.

6. James D. Thompson, ORGANIZATIONS IN ACTION (New York: McGraw-Hill, 1967), p. 67; see also his more detailed discussion of how these roles vary in routinization, power, and mobility, p. 110, passim. See also Philip S. Kronenberg, MICROPOLITICS AND PUBLIC PLANNING: A COMPARATIVE STUDY OF THE INTER-ORGANIZATIONAL POLITICS OF PLANNING, Ph.D. diss., University of Pittsburgh, 1969, esp. chap. 3.

7. G.L. Wamsley, "The Joint Chiefs of Staff: An Organizational Analysis," paper, Graduate School of Public and International Affairs, University of Pittsburgh, 1965, pp. 77-79.

8. Herbert Kaufman, THE FOREST RANGER: A STUDY IN ADMINISTRATIVE BEHAVIOR (Baltimore: Johns Hopkins Press, 1960), p. 214. See also Seidman, POLITICS, POSITION AND POWER, p. 114.

9. See similar point by Amitai Etzioni, MODERN ORGANIZATIONS (Englewood Cliffs, N.J.: Prentice-Hall, 1964), pp. 68-70.

10. For discussion of exchange and compliance theories, see Peter B. Clark and James Q. Wilson, "Incentive Systems: A Theory of Organizations," ADMINISTRATIVE SCIENCE QUARTERLY 6, no. 2 (September 1961), 129-66; Amitai Etzioni, A COMPARATIVE ANALYSIS OF COMPLEX ORGANIZA-

TIONS (New York: Free Press, 1961). All three, Wilson and Clark and Etzioni, deal with comparative compliance bases (how different kinds of organizations use different kinds of incentives). Their work can be derived from a more general analysis of exchange-incentive relations found in Chester Barnard, FUNCTIONS OF THE EXECUTIVE (Cambridge, Mass.: Harvard University Press, 1938); Simon et al., PUBLIC ADMINISTRATION; and Richard Emerson, "Power-Dependence Relations," AMERICAN SOCIOLOGICAL REVIEW 27 (February 1962): 31-40.

11. See Anthony Downs, INSIDE BUREAUCRACY (Boston: Little, Brown, 1967), pp. 224-26.

12. See Richard H. McCleery, POLICY CHANGE IN PRISON MANAGE-MENT (East Lansing, Mich.: Michigan State University, Governmental Research Bureau, 1957).

13. See D. Street, R. Vinter, and C. Perrow, ORGANIZATION FOR TREATMENT (New York: Free Press, 1966).

14. Samuel Huntington, "The Marasmus of the I.C.C.: The Commission, the Railroads and the Public Interest," YALE LAW JOURNAL 61, no. 4 (April 1952), 467-509.

15. The Hoover Commission, as quoted in Richard Fenno, THE PRESI-DENT'S CABINET (Cambridge, Mass.: Harvard University Press, 1959), p. 228.

16. Simon, Smithburg, and Thompson, PUBLIC ADMINISTRATION, p. 301.

17. A good beginning, though not applied directly to public organizations, is found in James D. Thompson, "Organizational Management Conflict," AD-MINISTRATIVE SCIENCE QUARTERLY 4, no. 4 (1960): 389-402.

18. Dean E. Mann, "The Selection of Federal Political Executives," AMER-ICAN POLITICAL SCIENCE REVIEW (March 1964), p. 81.

19. David T. Stanley, Dean E. Mann, James Doig, MEN WHO GOVERN (Washington, D.C.: The Brookings Institution, 1967), pp. 140-41.

20. Ibid., pp. 41-42.

21. For a discussion of this in the United States military, see Morris Janowitz, THE PROFESSIONAL SOLDIER (New York: Free Press, 1960), chap. 8.

22. Thompson, ORGANIZATIONS IN ACTION, p. 10. This entire section draws heavily on his excellent work, which we feel is the best synthesis that exists of a most diverse and inchoate field.

23. Louis Pondy, "Effects of Size, Complexity, and Ownership on Adminis-trative Intensity," ADMINISTRATIVE SCIENCE QUARTERLY 14, no. 1 (1969): 20-24.

24. Thompson, ORGANIZATIONS IN ACTION, pp. 43-44. See also Erving Goffman "On the Characteristics of Total Institutions," THE PRISON: STUD-IES IN INSTITUTIONAL ORGANIZATION AND CHANGE, ed. Donald R. Cressey (New York: Holt, Rinehart & Winston, 1961), chaps. 1-2.

25. Anthony Downs, INSIDE BUREAUCRACY, pp. 92-112. Downs also cites economy of scale as a factor in expansion.

26. Charles Perrow, ORGANIZATIONAL ANALYSIS: A SOCIOLOGICAL VIEW (Belmont, Calif.: Wadsworth, 1970), p. 65.

27. See the discussion of Lowi's typology in Chapter 2.

28. Thompson, ORGANIZATIONS IN ACTION, Chapter 5, pp. 51-65.

29. See U.S. GOVERNMENT ORGANIZATION MANUAL, 1965-66 (Washington, D.C.: Office of the Federal Register, U.S. Government Printing Office, 1966), pp. 396, 615.

29. Theodore A. Anderson and Seymour Warkov, "Organizational Size and Functional Complexity: A Study of Administration in Hospitals," AMERICAN SOCIOLOGICAL REVIEW 26, no. 1 (February 1961): 23-27. William A. Rushing, "The Effect of Industry Size and Division of Labor on Administration," ADMINISTRATIVE SCIENCE QUARTERLY 12, no. 2 (September 1967): 273-95.

30. James D. Thompson and Frederick L. Bates, "Technological Organization and Administration," ADMINISTRATIVE SCIENCE QUARTERLY 2, no. 3 (December 1957): 325-43. See also Benjamin Walter, "Internal Control Relations in Administrative Hierarchies," ADMINISTRATIVE SCIENCE QUARTERLY 11, no. 2 (September 1966): pp. 179-206.

31. See for example, Kaufman, THE FOREST RANGER; Herbert Simon, ADMINISTRATIVE BEHAVIOR, op. cit., Wamsley, SELECTIVE SERVICE AND A CHANGING AMERICA.

32. Wildavsky, "Politics of the Budgetary Process" (Boston: Little, Brown, 1964), pp. 2-3.

33. Wildavsky, ibid., passim.

34. "Innovation in Organizations: Notes Toward a Theory," in APPROACHES TO ORGANIZATIONAL DESIGN, ed. James D. Thompson (Pittsburgh: University of Pittsburgh Press, 1966), pp. 193-218.

Chapter 4
Squaring the Circle? The Unification
of Public Administration Theory

1. Gulick and Urwick, eds. Also Frederick W. Taylor, SCIENTIFIC MANAGEMENT (New York: Harper & Row, 1971).

2. Allen Schick, "The Road to PPB: The Stages of Budget Reform," PUBLIC ADMINISTRATION REVIEW 26, no. 4 (December 1966). Schick's article is so penetrating in analysis that it makes the stages clearer than they ever were to students and practitioners. Wildavsky is an exception to the above description. He has zeroed in on the political aspects of budgeting. One could say he has done so to the point of excluding their economic impact. Wildavsky,

"The Politics of the Budgetary Process" (Boston: Little, Brown, 1964). Also, his "The Political Economy of Efficiency: Cost-Benefit Analysis, Systems Analysis and Program Budgeting," PUBLIC ADMINISTRATION REVIEW 26 (1966).

3. John Pfiffner and Robert Presthus, PUBLIC ADMINISTRATION, 5th ed. (New York: Ronald Press, 1967), p. 257.

4. "Soviet Foreign Policy," in FOREIGN POLICY IN WORLD POLITICS, ed. Roy C. Macrides, 2d ed. (Englewood, N.J.: Prentice-Hall, 1962), pp. 168-86.

5. Conversations with Robert Donaldson, Vanderbilt University.

6. Dye, POLITICS, ECONOMICS AND PUBLIC; POLICY OUTCOMES IN THE AMERICAN STATES.

7. Theodore Lowi, "American Business, Public Policy, Case Studies & Political Theory," WORLD POLITICS XVI (July, 1964), 677-715.

8. Graham T. Allison, "Conceptual Models and the Cuban Missile Crisis," AMERICAN POLITICAL SCIENCE REVIEW 62 (September, 1969): 689-718.

9. U.S., Department of State, Bulletin 47, pp. 715-20.

10. Ibid.

11. Allison, op. cit.

12. Ibid., p. 698.

13. Ibid., pp. 708-709.

14. Allison, op. cit., p. 691.

15. For an analogous perspective see Norton E. Long, "Local Community as an Ecology of Games," AMERICAN JOURNAL OF SOCIOLOGY 64 (May, 1959), 251-61.

16. For detailed analysis and description of the "moves," see Wamsley, SELECTIVE SERVICE CHANGING AMERICA, especially chap. 7, or James W. Davis, Jr., and Kenneth Dolbeare, LITTLE GROUPS OF NEIGHBORS (Chicago: Markham, 1968), p. 000.

17. Allison, "Conceptual Models," p. 716.

Index